CONVERSATIONS
and COSMOPOLITANS

ALSO BY ROBERT RAVE

Waxed

Spin

ROBERT RAVE *and* JANE RAVE

CONVERSATIONS
and COSMOPOLITANS

Awkward Moments, Mixed Drinks,
and How a Mother and Son Finally
Shared Who They Really Are

ST. MARTIN'S GRIFFIN

NEW YORK

www.stmartins.com

Library of Congress Cataloging-in-Publication Data

Rave, Robert.
    Conversations and cosmopolitans : awkward moments, mixed drinks,
and how a mother and son finally shared who they really are /
Robert Rave and Jane Rave.—1st ed.
       p. cm.
    ISBN 978-0-312-55423-1 (alk. paper)
    1. Rave, Robert.   2. Mothers and sons.   3. Coming out (Sexual
orientation)   I. Rave, Jane.   II. Title.
    PS3618.A935Z46 2011
    813'.6—dc23
    [B]
                                                        2011026766

First Edition: November 2011

10 9 8 7 6 5 4 3 2 1

Dedicated to Ron Rave, whose fantastic storytelling is only outmatched by the size of his heart.

CONTENTS

CONTENTS

ACKNOWLEDGMENTS

Hem your blessings with thankfulness so they don't unravel.
—Author Unknown

Robert Rave would like to thank:

Bryan Jacobson, you were the one person to hear 90 percent of the stories in this book as they happened. You always made me keep my sense of humor through it all. I miss you, Queen. You may be gone, but I carry your laughter with me every day.

A debt of gratitude to my literary agent and all-around great guy, Jason Allen Ashlock. Your wisdom is only outmatched by your grace.

Sincere appreciation to my editor at St. Martin's Press, Sarah Johnson, who has left an indelible impression on everything that I write.

Thank you, thank you, thank you to Sally Richardson, Matthew Shear, John Murphy, Ann Day, and the sensationally talented and hard-working people at St. Martin's Press for believing in me.

Thanks to Elizabeth Newman and Michelle Weiner at CAA.

To Matt Walker and Joshua Carmichael Fearnley at Period Media.

To André Mello for your continued friendship and for reading everything I write before anyone else.

To Blaire Bercy, who listens to me for hours on end and tells me when to tone down the crazy . . . and when to turn it up.

To the incredibly generous authors who took the time to read this book and be kind enough to write something about it: Bryan Batt, Lance Bass, Robert Leleux, Heather McDonald, and Mishna Wolff.

To those who inspired, encouraged, and made me smile along the way: SuChin Pak, Scott Seviour, Richard Chung, Lisa Delcampo, Lance Bass, Marc Malkin, Jake Gant, Luigi Picarazzi, Jonathan Kruger, Jamie King, Rodney Ferrell, Harley Rodriguez, Jeremy Blacklow, Greg Baldwin, Jennifer Gill, Michelle Jubelirer, Jon Barrett, Peter Marc Jacobson, Paul Aaron, and Christopher Miele.

I've said it before, but thank *you*, the reader, for buying my books, taking the time to read them, and telling your friends. Thank you for your e-mails, Tweets, and Facebook messages. You continue to make my dreams a reality.

Jane Rave would like to thank:

First off, Robert thanked most of the people I had planned on thanking—but there are a few who deserve a second thank-you.

I would like to thank my editor at St. Martin's Press, Sarah Johnson, for all of her support and confidence in this book.

Thank you to St. Martin's Press, and in particular: Sally Richardson, Matthew Shear, John Murphy, and Ann Day.

Thanks to my agent (yeah, that's pretty fun to say), Jason Allen Ashlock.

I'd also like to thank my family for their support of me, and of their brother, Robert.

Thanks to Ron for always being there for me, especially through this whole process of writing a book that was often daunting and scary. He is my biggest fan and the love of my life.

Growing up, whenever I gave my mother a smart remark, she would warn me that a smack was imminent by saying that I was "testing the waters."

My response to this day has remained the same: "Lady, I'm kissing the bottom of the pool."

Introduction

So the big question is, "Why write a book like this together?" My mother is quite happy in her life as a mom and grandma and she's certainly not looking to achieve stardom or huge cash rewards. We are a strong family, just trying to deal with living and loving life in our own way, like millions of families around the world. As for me, I'm not a fan of sharing my biggest insecurities with the world.

We're not therapists, and we're not looking to transform your life overnight. We are, however, a mother and son who have lived through a life-changing experience, one that we hope you can learn from. We decided to write this book to both enlighten and entertain in the hope that other families facing similar life-changing issues will begin a discussion in their own homes. This book is a collection of conversations my mother and I had—some on the phone, others in person, and on a few occasions, online.

The collection actually started fifteen years ago, when I sent my parents a monumental letter making my mother aware of the fact that she wouldn't be going shopping for baby clothes with a daughter-in-law anytime in the foreseeable future. Not surprisingly, my mother had several worries when I came out. In fact, she thought that she was about to lose me to some sort of deep, dark underworld of promiscuity, drugs, and leather. Sure, she could sympathize with my sister over her boyfriends or even my brother with girlfriends, because she'd once been there herself. She knew how to be a shoulder to cry on for my sister's breakups, and she also understood the excitement of new love (heterosexual love, that is). Somehow my mother feared that I was going to disappear into a world whose rules she didn't comprehend. Even more, she feared that she'd no longer be needed.

It was also during these conversations that I learned a great deal about myself and my mother. So often as children we never truly know our parents. I feel blessed to say that I'm one of the fortunate ones who does.

Since then, this little collection grew. Later, it would show my mother and me what an enormously empowering process living in the truth can be. Sometimes my opinion conflicts with hers, as you will see in the "Mama Says" sections. We know that every story has three sides to it—your side, their side, and the truth. Our truth rests comfortably somewhere in between.

Some conversations are laugh-out-loud funny. Some are painfully uncomfortable. However, they are all real. Names have been changed to protect the innocent *and* the guilty.

Take from this book whatever you need to open a dialogue with your own mother, son, father, daughter, brother, sister, or best friend. Of course in retrospect and many years later, I'm mortified at some of these stories, but at the end of the day if it helps to get you talking, then sharing my embarrassment with you is well worth it. Our greatest hope is that you will begin to know one another in a new and honest way. With any luck, you'll be enjoying your own *Conversations and Cosmopolitans* soon.

PART ONE:

The Letter (Coming Out Via the U.S. Mail)

CHAPTER ONE

The End

Graduation day for a gay-in-training who's decided
to come out to his conservative Midwestern parents

Within one month of moving to New York, I sat down at my
computer and began drafting what I affectionately refer to as "the
message of honesty and love." I poured my heart and soul into this
letter, offering answers to every question my parents might have
regarding my sexuality. At twenty-one, I viewed it as a great literary work and fantasized that one day, years after my death, it would
be framed, like the letters of Virginia Wolfe.

However, my mother diminishes this great literary feat, referring
to it simply as "the gay letter." That's my mother: sweet but definitely
to the point. I've reprinted the letter here with its original typos and
grammatical errors, all of which she's pointed out to me.

Hey guys this is the hardest thing I have had to do in my life.
This letter is not something I ever wanted to write or never
wanted to have to deal with myself. For the past 21 years I
kept thinking that it would pass or that things would change I
think I have been fooling myself and I can no longer lie to you
because I love you both so much and feel that we are extremely close to each other that it pains me more not to tell
you than to keep it to myself. I might as well just lay it on the
line: I am gay.

You have to understand that just as I typed that I am
actually welling up because I have never officially acknowledged to myself in black and white or let alone to another

person. I know this is going to be very, very painful for you to accept your hopes and dreams for me may seem like they have disappeared in many ways. Believe me, they have not. I am the same Robert, Bob, Bobby, Berto that you raised so well. I guess I am writing this letter because I am much better expressing myself through the written word sometimes as opposed to physically saying it. I get all jumbled and nervous. Plus, I wanted to give you time to think about this and react and mourn and go through all the necessary emotions and then come talk to me about it when your ready.

I don't expect you to understand or necessary accept it right away. It has taken me 21 years to accept. The best thing I could think of to do is to give you some basic question and answers that you are probably already thinking of that you know where I am coming from instead of me just rambling on and on and making much sense.

Are you sure you are gay? Is it just a phase? Is it the way you were raised?

Well I am 100% positive that I am gay. I have tried to date women and be sexual with them but it just never connected or clicked no matter how hard I tried or how many times I tried. I just am not sexually attracted to them. For so many years I just kept lying to myself and telling myself that it would pass and the attraction would come and I just inevitably was forcing something that wasn't there and after awhile I felt like I was headed for a breakdown because I was feeling so tor- mented inside by the lies I would have to tell myself and to others. There were so many nights starting about 11 or 12 where I would go to bed praying that when I woke up that I wouldn't be gay. I did this almost every night until about age 19 when I realized either God has fallen asleep or it wasn't

going to happen. I remember wishing that I would be anything but gay. I remember saying I rather be physically
handicapped then gay. As much as I thought that my being gay
would pass, the stronger it became the older I got.

Was the way I raised have anything to do with my being gay?
  ABSOLUTELY NOT. I have always been my own person
and have chose my own interests thanks to the freedom that
you both have given to me. But with all the choices and
opportunities that you both have given me the choice of my
sexuality was not one of them. I wish it was because I never
would have chosen this. I would never have chosen to be
made fun of, discriminated against, laughed at, and ridiculed.
This is something that I have known from a very early age.

Is this why you moved to NYC?
  NO. NO. NO. My reasons for moving out to New York
are because I want to be in the city that doesn't sleep and
where I can thrive on the energy and life of a city. I want to
live in a place where there is something new you can do
everyday. I moved to New York to pursue my dreams. It is
very frightening and exciting for me to say the least. Not only
with me being up in the air about a job but with keeping this
secret that I couldn't do it no longer. I felt that if I didn't tell
you in the next couple of months I would have seriously had a
breakdown with all of the stress that has been escalating and
that is no exaggeration. To say that I had a lot on my mind
would be a grave over-generalization.

Why tell us now?
  Good question. I don't know why this week or this day or
this particular year. I just knew that I couldn't continue to lie

to you anymore. I have been extremely open with you about every other aspect of my life. This guilt has torn me apart and I couldn't stand the sleepless nights anymore.

I didn't like lying to you about another major aspect of who I am. It hurts me so much to know that this letter is hurting you both. The last thing I want to do is hurt you by all this. I have so much love and respect for both of you that the last thing I want to do is hurt you by this. That is why I couldn't bear to see the expressions on both of your faces. It would literally crush me. But for the last couple years it no longer was a question of if I told you, it was more of a question of when. For my own mental welfare, it was time to tell you. It is so hard to do but in some ways as I am typing this it feels very cathartic and up lifting that lies about this major aspect of my life can now end.

Does anybody else know?

NO. I knew that you two should be the first since you two are the most important people in my life. As far as me wanting to broadcast it to the world, its not going to happen at least not right now. I have to deal with this too. My immediately family is the only people that I am really concerned about it. I don't think that aunts, uncles, cousins, and grandparents really need to know at this point. I mean if they ask I won't lie nor do I expect you to lie, but somehow I don't see it coming up. I am not of those gay people you see on TV or in the paper with their pink flags and marching in parades although I do believe gay people deserve the same rights as the rest of the human race.

Anyway, one the reasons I never really considered myself gay was because of the images that I saw on television were not me. I am not one of those images that the media was representing on the news etc. However, as more "normal" gay people came out and lead normal lives it makes me feel a little better that the tide is changing with the perception. But back to the question, none of my friends know with the exception of Laurie whom I had to tell because I really needed someone to talk to desperately. For the rest of my friends, I am sure I will lose 75% of them when they find out. I am in no rush to tell them in fact the friends that I truly care about most of them I will tell them myself, the others if they find out won't come from me. I just don't want to be the embarrassment of our family. I don't want to be the one everyone whispers about and don't want to bring shame to you both. Although, I know that people will whisper and judge and will discriminate against me. That will be my cross to bear I suppose. We all have them. All I ask is for your continued love and eventually your support and understanding and maybe ultimately your acceptance.

Well, these were just a few questions that I could think of that you might have but I am sure you will have many more and I know that you are probably in complete and utter shock. I am so sorry to put you through this but I just couldn't lie to you anymore. I want our relationship to be open and honest. Call me after you have had time to take it all in. I am not expecting alot and I am sure it will be rough. Please know that I love you both so very much to my core and no matter what, I am proud to be your son as I hope that no matter what gay or straight your proud to be my parents. I love you and I hope to hear from you soon.

Love,
Robert

Mama Says

It was a regular Tuesday morning. I got up around five thirty, had my breakfast, and read our local paper. It looked like it was going to be like any other day in Bloomington, Illinois. My husband, Ron, went to work early that morning for a meeting. I ran some errands—the bank, grocery store, and then a quick stop at my mom's house for coffee—and finally returned home around twelve thirty and sat down at my kitchen table for lunch. Just as I was about to take a bite of my sandwich, our dog, Barney, started barking like he was possessed. It could only mean trouble. But this trouble was in the form of the mailman. I put down my sandwich and grabbed my overweight, temperamental shih tzu before I had a lawsuit on my hands and made my way to the mailbox.

I thumbed through the stack of mail and made a note to myself to dispose of the credit card bill before my husband saw it. (Yes, even I have a vice.) I got to the middle of the stack and saw that there was a letter from Berto. I was excited to see it, because he had been in New York for only a few months and he was already sending me an update. The letter was unusually thick, but I didn't think much of it. In retrospect, I was a little surprised to get an actual handwritten letter as opposed to an e-mail. He was very big with the e-mails. All I thought at the time was, "Great, he has a lot to tell me about New York City."

Well, guess what? He did have *a lot* to tell me, just not about New York.

I went back to the table and excitedly opened the letter, expecting to read some fun stories about his new job working at a PR firm. As I read the first paragraph, I was in complete shock. I read it over again, and the words didn't change. The neatly formatted letter was filled with paragraphs, but all I kept seeing was *Mom and Dad, I'm gay*.

I thought I had better keep reading. I couldn't even imagine what else he might have to tell me. After reading it through, my heart ached so much for my youngest son. He was so far away, and I couldn't see his face to let him know it was okay. I felt so much sadness for him that I didn't even realize that I had begun to cry until the tears began hitting the paper. I cried not for myself, but for my son. He was alone and didn't feel he could tell me face-to-face. Then again, if I had been in his shoes, would I have been able to tell my mom? I guess we are all different when it comes to the dramas in our lives. I suppose I am not sure what I would have done.

I worried about the hard times he would face for the rest of his life. I watched the news, and I saw how people viewed gays and lesbians. I also didn't live in a big city, where one is exposed to gay people on a daily basis. I heard the nasty comments that people made, and what hurt most was knowing I couldn't protect him from the abuse and discrimination that was yet to come.

I worried he would go through it alone trying to find his true identity. The more I thought about it, the more I realized he knew who he was and could start getting on with living his life. He didn't need to be worrying about me.

I was a middle-aged stay-at-home mom, and I never really felt as if I knew who I was, but here was my son, who knew for sure who he was. I thought, maybe this experience would force me to find out who I was, too.

It never even occurred to me to worry about what other people would think. I had never worried about it prior to this, so why would I start now? I'd leave that to the TV movies of the week. This was one of my children, and he needed me right now.

I knew what my next move had to be, no matter how difficult. I called Ron at work and interrupted his meeting. All I would tell him was to get home right away because we needed to talk. I'm sure he wondered what was going on, especially when he heard the quiver in my voice, but I thought he should read what I now refer to as "the gay letter" himself. A big part of me wanted to call Robert right away and tell him it was okay; if he could handle being gay, so could I. But my husband and I have always worked as a team when it comes to our kids, so I needed him to read it before I made a move.

While I waited for Ron to get home, I composed myself and tried to keep busy. I cleaned up the kitchen, and then I took Barney out even though I had just done so twenty minutes earlier.

I sat at the table and stared at my sandwich. How couldn't I have seen this coming? You would think, considering how close Robert and I are, that I would have known or at least suspected. Every talk show I ever watched said the mother always knows, either subconsciously or consciously. Not me—I didn't have a clue. Robert hadn't been the stereotypical gay guy I'd seen on the news or in the movies. He'd always been "all boy."

Finally, I heard the garage door go up.

CHAPTER TWO

The Waiting Game

Things to do in NYC when you are
on the verge of a nervous breakdown

It had been only three hours since I put the letter in the mail, but I was desperate for some kind of affirmation. Okay, let's face it: I was just plain desperate. I saw a copy of the *Village Voice* sitting on my kitchen table. (I use the term "kitchen" loosely, as I lived in a Manhattan studio apartment. I don't know how many of your friends can reach across their bed and put their empty Tostitos bag on their kitchen table.) I feverishly thumbed through the *Voice* in the hopes of finding something to calm my nerves. It was too early to start drinking. I didn't do drugs. I had already gone to the gym and worked off my nervous energy for two hours. I ran so much on that treadmill that I still had the sliding sensation as I walked to my bathroom.

I didn't see much in the paper. I turned to the masseuse listings in the back, but those were the kind that offered "release," and I was in no position to call one of them (for financial reasons more than moral ones).

Then, all of a sudden, something leapt off page eighty-seven. It was a listing of all the self-help meetings taking place in Manhattan. That was it—the answer to my prayers! If I couldn't deal with my own problems, at least I could wallow in everyone else's *and* get the affirmation I so frantically wanted. At the very least, I could take comfort that there were people worse off than me, as hard as that was to believe.

I scanned the pages of every "recovering" this and that and realized my choices were limited due to the Labor Day weekend:

Substance Abuse? No, too boring. The truth was I needed a few drinks, and I didn't want to feel guilty because of it.

Sexual Counseling: Uniting Sex and Spirit? I was twenty-one, and the closest thing I had come to uniting sex and spirit was screaming, "Oh, God" in the throes of passionate copulating (which was usually over within minutes). No, that wouldn't do, either. I had visions of people sitting around naked being taped for *Real Sex* episode 148 on HBO. I was not ready for that kind of superstardom just yet.

Anxiety and Depression? Of course I had anxiety, for God's sake. I had just written a letter to my parents telling them I was a full-on gay boy. They could turn their backs on me forever. They could renounce me and wipe out my entire existence. They could try to send me to one of those gay outreach programs where they try to make you straight. *Oh, God! How in the hell are they going to react?* The anticipation was driving me over the edge. But I didn't need to go to this one; I just don't think I could relate to those neurotic types.

I guessed that maybe these meetings wouldn't be helpful after all. I secretly wished that one of them would give me the peace I was looking for and the hope that my parents would accept me. I threw the paper back on the table, and like a verse from a Deepak Chopra book, fate tapped me on the shoulder, and I saw the answer to my prayers.

Gamblers Anonymous.

It was eleven thirty, and there was a noon meeting at St. Mark's Church in the East Village. If I hurried, I could still make it. I wasn't quite sure yet how a Gamblers Anonymous meeting was going to help me with the situation with my parents, but I could probably pick up some good blackjack tips or a tip on this evening's Knicks game. I was willing to give it a try.

I breezed into the basement of the church at exactly 12:05. The room was damp and poorly lit. Apparently these odds-makers didn't want to be seen, either. In the corner sat three overweight men that reeked of cigars. What I mistook for a betting playbook was the sign-in sheet. I gave myself 10-1 odds that I'd stay the full hour and a half.

As the cigar smokers leaned into the light to sign in, I was thankful the room was dim. I felt like I was hanging out on the set of *Roseanne*, but thankfully not everyone at the meeting looked like John Goodman. At the opposite end sat a very rigid Wall Street–type woman dressed in a black suit and sneakers with racing forms from Belmont hanging out of her purse. I moved closer to her. She seemed normal enough except for her poor fashion choice (sneakers with a suit), but I was willing to overlook it because I'm open to new experiences.

Some guy named Larry, who from what I gathered was either the group leader or an overeager self-help fanatic, quickly welcomed me to the meeting. It was a sorry lot, and although I was likely the only one who could safely say I'd be able to overcome gambling in my life, I decided to stay and see what I could learn. Larry nodded at a man that sat to my left. He was slightly overweight and wore a workman's shirt with his name, Al, sewn above his chest. He looked like a true man's man, a real tough guy.

"Big Al, would you like to share?" Larry asked.

Big Al cleared his throat, took a deep breath, and then began his story. "Within the last fourteen months, the bank took my house, my car was repossessed, and my wife left me after twelve years of marriage because I used the only money we had left for groceries to bet on St. John's. It would've been the biggest payoff I had all week if the motherfucker didn't sink a three-pointer. She now lives at a shelter with my seven-year-old son."

He had to be putting us on. He began to cry as he talked about his wife. "I first met my wife in the seventh grade. She was my first and only crush, and I knew she'd be with me forever . . ."

My cynicism turned to sympathy, and I began to think about my first crush. His name was Marco Jacobs. He was beautiful, athletic, masculine, and had the best smile I'd ever seen. He was an Abercrombie & Fitch ad before the Abercrombie & Fitch ads. He was Bruce Weber's wet dream.

At fourteen, I wasn't sure what it was I felt for him, but I knew I wanted to be with him every waking hour. He was so cool. I went to our local sports club just so I could be around him. I played basketball for hours—drenched with sweat, legs wobbly, and arms so tired I could barely hold the ball—but it was all worth it. I was sure he felt the same way about me. Come on, his name was Marco. He *had* to be gay!

I didn't know what to do or how to express that I liked him (I mean *really* liked him). When we weren't playing basketball or debating whose lyrics were more powerful, Guns N' Roses or Run DMC, we passed notes in between classes. They usually went something like this:

Marco,

What's up??? Not much with me, I'm sitting in Mr. Miller's Geometry class bored out of my f$*cking mind. I'm psyched to hang out later. Are we going to play hoops? Maybe we can go for pizza afterwards? I want to see Lethal Weapon this weekend, do you want to go? Let's hang out this weekend. Do you have plans? I don't. Okay, I better go, he's looking over at me.

Later,

Robert

His response:

Hey. Not much. I'm playing basketball with Steve after school. You can come if you want. We might need a sixth man if Josh doesn't show up. I'm going to the movie with Natalie. I can't hang this weekend.

Marco

PS. Don't give me any more notes in the hall dude, it's kinda gay.

I was too scared to tell Marco that I wanted to be with him forever. And it wasn't even a sexual thing; I just idolized him so much. Like most gay teenagers, I was forced to hide my real feelings, and I thought I was doing a good job of it, until Steve and Josh called me a fag for following Marco around. Normally I would have blown it off, but this was at lunch during a class field trip to the Museum of Science and Industry in Chicago. For the rest of our tour, everyone, even some of the girls, called me a fag. Even Bridget Mutler, the biggest geek in all of All Saints, called me a "fudge packer" as she laughed with bits of brownie stuck in her braces, making her look like she had just eaten poop. Apparently I packed it, but even though she ate it, I was still the worse of the two.

I did all I could not to cry in front of them. I rode the bus home sitting next to David Weller. David's claim to fame was that he could turn his eyelids inside out and pick his nose and eat whatever came out. And even *he* didn't want to be next to me, a fag.

Marco never spoke to me again.

I never told my parents. I didn't want to give them the slightest indication that I could be gay, because that was too terrifying. So I went home and put a smile on my face and pretended the Museum of Science and Industry was the coolest field trip ever. I went up-stairs and picked up the phone to dial Marco to tell him it was all just a big joke and that Steve, Josh, and I were in on it together. I stared at the phone for what seemed like hours, twirling the long phone cord and staring into the green illuminated numbers on the receiver. The truth was, I wanted it to be a joke. I didn't want it to be real. God forbid I said it out loud, because once I said it to my-self, it was my reality. I gently put the phone down, sat on the edge of my bed, and began to cry. From that moment on, I knew I was definitely different from everyone else, and I'd spend the next eight years doing whatever it took to hide it.

I looked at Big Al in the dim light of that basement and realized he had secrets, much as I did. As I sat in the folding chair, I surveyed the room long and hard. I definitely didn't have a gambling prob-lem. (Who was I kidding? You can't gamble without any money.) I thought I wanted to hear about how pathetic and miserable these strangers' lives were and how my problems paled in comparison. But I realized that maybe I wasn't so different from this group after all. Al's secrets had cost him everything he cared about and loved, and they tore him up inside. Yet he was willing to risk everything just so no one would discover his secret. He was just like me. And now, as I waited for my mother's response, I was bracing for the same outcome.

But if there's one thing my mother always taught me, it's that sometimes it's good to bet on the underdog—*even if the odds are 10-1.*

Mama Says

I had time to pull it together before Ron got home, or at least that's what I thought. When he walked in, he could tell right away that I'd been crying.

"What is it?"

A million things ran through my mind. How was I going to say it? I couldn't just blurt it out.

"Hi, dear! Your son's gay. Coffee?" No, too Stepford Wife–like.

Maybe a more serious approach. "Honey, what I am about to tell you could destroy your life as you know it." That could work . . . if I were a character on *Days of Our Lives*.

He was growing impatient; I had to tell him something.

"Well," he asked, "what the hell's going on?"

Then, strangely, a feeling of calm swept over me. I handed him the letter without saying a word and put on a pot of coffee. (I thought that was a nice touch.)

I knew it'd be hard for him. Robert was our youngest boy, and like any parents, we had certain ideas of what we wanted for our child— and this was probably the last thing Ron was hoping for. We'd always said the most important thing was for our kids to be happy, but I hadn't thought that meant this. As I watched him read, I worried about the pain he must have been feeling. He finally got to the end, and he looked at me. I hated to see the hurt in his eyes. Finally, after a few minutes, he spoke.

"What's the big deal?" he said.

Clearly, he had glossed over the "gay" part of the letter, or at the very least chosen *not* to see it.

"Are you in denial?" I asked.

"About?" he said, puzzled.

"Your son just told you he was gay in that letter," I said sympathetically.

"Yeah, and?" he said.

I wasn't sure what shocked me more, Robert's letter or my husband's reaction. It was a pleasant surprise. Not that I ever expected Ron to disown Robert because of it, but I didn't expect him to be so . . . *okay* with it. My husband had been an All-American in high school football and lettered in four other sports; he'd played college football and was in a fraternity.

"Yeah, and are you sure you are comfortable with this?" I asked.

"There were times I wondered if he was gay," he said very nonchalantly. "Now I know for sure," he said. "Coffee?"

What? Not only was he more okay with it than me, but now he was using *my* prepared lines! I was dumbfounded.

I was still in shock. Ron sipped his coffee. "At the end of the day, does it really matter? He's our son. He was before the letter. Why should it change now?"

This was why I married this man.

As we sat at the table drinking our coffee, the first thing we wanted to do was call Robert. I knew he'd be freaking out. Either that or he'd have locked himself in his apartment waiting for our call. We wanted to get through to him right away to reassure him of our love. You hear of so many horror stories about teenagers, and even young men and women, killing themselves over something like this. While we knew Robert wasn't the type to go to such extremes, we also knew it was essential to speak to him right away.

I dialed his number, eager to tell him how much we loved him.

I could just imagine him sitting in that studio apartment with one hand on the phone the entire weekend. Poor thing.

I put the phone to my ear and was ready to pour out my heart and soul . . . when I heard a busy signal. I tried again . . . and then again . . . and yet again. I sat at that damn kitchen table with my husband for over an hour and a half. Who in the hell could he be talking to for so long? And he better not have taken it off the hook, or he's *really* going to get a talking to.

That little shit.

CHAPTER THREE

ClairBOYant

Coming out to a complete stranger hoping they'll
predict a glimpse of happiness in your future for
$3.99 a minute (see also: *verbal Xanax*)

One thing I learned during my first self-help meeting was that people have a fundamental need for connection in its most basic form. I
still wasn't feeling connected, and I couldn't talk to anybody because
I was very new to New York. Who was I going to ramble on to? I
thought about calling my childhood friends, but last I had heard, one
was due to give birth at any moment, the other was studying for the
bar exam, and another, a former roommate, had always had a philosophy of "Adam and Eve, not Adam and Steve." My choices, therefore,
were a baby's mama, a soon-to-be lawyer, and a homophobe. Which
one would you choose? Exactly. That's what I thought. So I did what
I swore I would never do.

Let me preface this by saying that I'd never considered myself a
smart guy. I'd done fairly well in school, I'd traveled, and I had
a decent job at a small theater PR company. But all my strength and
intelligence apparently went down the toilet when, in an effort to
make that all-important connection, I reached out and touched
someone named "Ms. Cleo."

Unfortunately, I didn't have the great fortune to speak with little-
known psychic Ms. Cleo herself. No, Ms. Cleo was far too busy tend-
ing to her legion of devoted disciples. I settled for the discount Cleo,
because, after all, the rent was due. I dialed, and after I navigated
through the endless ads for 900 numbers, I finally reached a live person, who asked for my credit card information. I hesitated slightly,
and the phone operator could smell my fear. "Look, honey," she said

in a thick Jamaican accent. "You are getting a reading for almost nothing. Where else could you get a reading for $3.99?" She neglected to mention it was per minute.

"Okay," I said, wanting some sort of affirmation that coming out to my parents had ultimately been the best thing to do.

"Hold for credit card authorization," she said in a now-morphing Jamaican-Brooklyn accent. "You are all set. Let me transfer you to your shaman," she said.

"My what? What the hell is 'sure man'?"

I was twenty-one, raised in a small town in the Midwest. With her thick accent, that's what I thought she'd said. How was I supposed to know a shaman was another word for a spiritual Zen-master?

"Ms. Cleo's spiritual line of wisdom. Shaman Debbie speaking. Your date of birth, please?"

Wait a second. My shaman's name was Debbie? Call me crazy, but the name Debbie didn't scream all-knowing soothsayer to me. Debbie seemed more like someone who worked the overnight shift at Denny's.

"June 10, 1974," I responded.

"One moment, please," she answered, and then she put me on hold for what seemed like years. I began to doodle on a piece of paper, thinking about my parents and their reaction to my letter. I walked around the apartment and tried to take my mind off it.

Fifteen minutes passed, and still no Debbie. At first I thought I'd been disconnected, but while I was on hold, bells chimed every so often, clearly to remind callers they were in fact still on hold and not actually brain dead. I refused to hang up. If I called back, I would be charged $15.99, since it would be considered a new call and, damn it, I needed some reassurance that things were going to work out for me. Yet I needed something to pass the time.

I tried everything. I turned on the computer and quickly shut it down in case my parents were online and started instant messaging or, even worse, if they saw me online and ignored me. I turned on the TV. Shockingly, I gravitated toward Lifetime. It was my luck that Lifetime was showing a true-life film starring Patty Duke in which her character investigates the death of her gay son in the military. I suddenly imagined my mother watching the docudrama while reading my letter.

"Hello? Hello?" I heard her repeat.

"Oh, hi. I didn't hear the chimes end," I said with a laugh. Debbie didn't think it was so funny, as she quickly cut me off.

"Anyway," she barked.

"Sorry," I muttered. I was being chastised by some fake shaman. I realized I had much bigger problems than simply telling my parents I was gay.

"For June tenth people, life clearly has its ups and downs. The more successful born on this day manage to synthesize and reconcile opposites . . . happy and sad, manic and depressed, funny and tragic. The less successful can be driven crazy by pendulum swings from light to dark and back again . . ."

This sounded strangely familiar to me, but I couldn't place my finger on why exactly. I let her continue.

"Clarify what is troubling you. Beware of escapism, whether it is into the world or out of it, and also of looking for your other half in someone else. Strive to integrate your actions and your fantasies."

"Excuse me, Shaman Debbie?"

"What is it?" she said, irritated.

"Did you just turn the page?"

"No, I don't know what you are talking about."

"I clearly heard you turn a page."

"No, I didn't," she snapped. "The tenth card of the Major Arcana is the Wheel of Fortune, which signifies a reversal in fortune and teaches that there is nothing permanent except change . . ."

While she continued to read, I walked to my bookshelf and

started throwing books onto the bed. Mind you, I was still being charged.

"Those ruled by the number one tend to be ambitious, but June tenth people can often manifest this drive subtly directing—"

"Others from behind the scenes?" I interrupted. There was a long pause. "Yeah, that's what I thought. I have *The Secret Language of Birthdays*, too. Ironically enough, I got it for, what else, my birthday."

Silence still.

"Why don't you just tell me what the hell you called for in the first place?" Her accent had suddenly changed from Jamaican Shaman to Montgomery Housewife.

I was suddenly at a loss for words. "Umm . . ."

"Look, honey, you might as well tell me. You've already paid all this money," she insisted.

"Fine," I said. "I sent my parents a letter telling them I was gay," I said nervously. "And now I'm freaking out!"

"In a letter? What the hell do you expect? Why would you send them a letter?"

"Uh, Debbie? Could we go less judgmental and a little more constructive? That'd be really helpful to me. Thanks."

"Sorry, honey. Well, what's the problem?" she asked.

"Well, what if they abandon me? I've heard the nightmarish stories. I know a guy whose dad had a heart attack when he found out! I don't want that on my conscience!"

"And what makes you think your dad will have a heart attack when he finds out? Does he have a history of heart problems?"

"No. Well, not that I know of. And my mother? How will it affect her? I'm the baby of the family. She's just waiting for me to get married—I can feel it!"

"When was the last time she asked you about getting married?" she asked.

"It's been awhile."

"And girlfriends?" she quizzed.

"Not since my freshman year of college," I confessed.

"Honey, she knows. Whether she realizes it or not, she knows on some level. This letter is no surprise to them," she quipped.

"Really?" I said solemnly.

"Yes, and guess what? You'll be fine," she said.

"I don't know, but—"

"But nothing. Hang up the damn phone"—her voice suddenly went back to her crazy shaman speak—"and call them! Be a man!"

"I guess you're right. Thank you, Debbie. You are awesome! This was money well spent." Debbie made me feel better so it was worth the money, but despite her advice from the other side, I couldn't work up the nerve to call home.

"Mm-hmm," I heard her mutter. "Go get 'em," she said.

"Hey, Debbie, by the way, do you think there's any way I can get a discount on this reading since I caught you reading out of the book?"

Suddenly, in a robotic voice, Shaman Debbie chanted, "Thank you for calling Ms. Cleo. Good-bye."

At this point, I was less scared of what my parents would say and more scared of my upcoming credit card bill.

Mama Says

Ms. Cleo? Seriously. I thought Robert was joking when he told me this story. I actually had to laugh out loud. "Come on. I taught you better than that," I said.

"What do you mean by 'taught me better than that'? You like psychics," he said.

"But Ms. Cleo?" I said.

"Um, yeah?" he said.

"It's ridiculous," I said.

As I'm sure you've already figured out, Robert has a constant need to know that everything is fine. I think there might be some slight OCD there, but I'm not really sure. I'm not a doctor. It shouldn't have come as a total surprise to me that he reached out to a psychic hotline, but what I *was* surprised about was that he chose to go with one from television. If he was going that route, at the very least, he should have called psychic Sylvia Browne.

Obviously, sometimes it's easier to tell a stranger everything. Being gay and in the closet is not easy and revealing it to the ones you love is hard. If that's what he needed Debbie for, then who cares who he spoke to? If she was a good listener, then it was well worth it.

I told him I think I should get a 1-900 number as well. Maybe I'd make some extra money to help pay the bill for his psychic.

Needless to say he wasn't amused.

CHAPTER FOUR
Solophobia

My parents' fear of their son ending up alone (but it has nothing, I mean NOTHING, to do with his commitment issues)

Let's face it. The world is changing. We in the human race don't like people. If it were up to me, I'd prefer not to have any human contact with anyone. (Okay, dogs are fine.) My love of my fellow man has been replaced by my love of technology. Thankfully, technology has given me the option of avoiding everyone altogether.

So when the phone rang two days after I spoke to Shaman Debbie, I seriously debated avoiding all contact with other human beings from then on. Then again, technology and my mother weren't the best of friends. My heart immediately sank into my shoes. The phone rang two more times. The machine went off, then the beep.

"Hi," I heard my mom say faintly. I could hear sniffles in the background. This was alarming, since she wasn't typically a crier. At that moment, my whole body became warm, as if I'd just stepped into a hot bath. *Say something!* I thought. I froze. Oh shit. My mind jumped to all the possibilities. Most of all, I feared it wasn't going to be the life-affirming call I was hoping for.

I said hello as cheerfully as I could, as if I didn't have the slightest idea why she was calling me. When I didn't hear her respond, I thought the worst. Until I realized that I hadn't actually picked up the phone.

I quickly grabbed it and said, "Yes! Hello. What are you guys up to? Did you see the Cubs game?" I was clamoring for useless conversation. Nothing could have prepared me for what they were about to say.

"Well, we got your letter," I heard my mom say. The niceties went out the window. They dug in right away.

"Yeah, I'm glad you did," I said. Before they could get a word out, I immediately began spewing. "I hope I answered all of your questions, because I really just felt that was the best way to do things and I wanted to let you know again that being gay was not my reason for moving to New York. I really hope you'll understand why I want to stay . . ."

I wouldn't shut up. When I was a kid, my parents would often refer to this affliction as "diarrhea of the mouth." I no longer felt as if I was talking about myself, but a friend of mine instead. I had become Whitney Houston. I'm sure you've seen her do it before. In TV interviews, whenever Whitney's feeling hot under the collar (or, in her case, flop sweat), she starts referring to herself in the third person. "No, Diane, Whitney doesn't do crack. Crack is cheap and I'm not cheap!" Or, my personal favorite, "Don't mess with Whitney!" I fell victim to it during this conversation, but I stopped short of saying, "No, Dad, Robert doesn't sleep with girls. Girls are cheap!"

I finally had to stop and take a breath, and I could hear my mom fighting back tears. "I don't want you to be upset," I said. "This is for me to deal with. I'm still the same person," I added emphatically.

"We know," my dad said.

"We just don't want you to end up alone," my mom interrupted.

Huh? Alone? Of all the possible things there were for them to worry about—AIDS, discrimination, drug and alcohol addiction—*my* parents were worried about me not finding a boyfriend. This was unbelievable.

"What do you mean?" I asked, surprised.

"The only gay people we know have always been alone," she said, her voice breaking.

"We don't want you to be alone for the rest of your life," my dad said quietly. This was one reaction that Ricki Lake hadn't prepared me for. Now it was my turn to give a long pause. Then I remembered.

"There are gay couples that you know of," I said confidently. "What about Gary and Gary? You built them their first house together, and they've been together for years," I said.

"Actually, Gary L. died a year ago, and now it's just Gary B. in that big house all by himself," my dad said solemnly.

"What about the lesbians?" I shot back. "You've built a lot of houses for lesbians over the years," I argued. "What about Marie and Colleen?"

"Colleen left Marie for the women's volleyball coach at the university," my mom answered. *ARGH!*

"Listen, this is not the issue here. The point is that I'm gay. I could be alone if I was straight. What's the big deal?"

My mother was crying again, making me worry that finding my soul mate was going to be much harder than I had anticipated. "We know we aren't going to be here forever, and we want to make sure all of our kids are happy and have someone to share their lives with, and from the extremely little bit that we know about gay life, most of them end up alone," she said again.

Wow. She'd hit me with the one-two punch. First, their mortality, and second, the prospect of being single and gay for the rest of my life. I was only twenty-one. I couldn't fully digest either one. For the rest of the conversation, I was pretty much silent. I don't think I realized exactly what it meant to be gay. Hell, I hadn't even thought about being gay and alone for the rest of my life. At that point, I would've been happy to go out on a date.

Mark Twain said this about mothers: "My mother had a great deal of trouble with me, but I think she enjoyed it." This has been the relationship with my mother my entire life.

Mama Says

After talking to Robert and letting him know we loved him anyway, I think he felt somewhat relieved that he didn't have to pretend anymore with the people he loved most. His dad and I felt the same: Robert was our son, and being gay really didn't matter. How we would tell his brother and sister was up to him.

He sort of panicked when we asked him how he would do this, and I spoke up and told him I would tell them and he insisted I show them the letter. As painful as I knew it would be to do, I agreed to do it the following week. At that moment, the most important thing for us was to make sure our son knew we loved him and would always be there for him . . . no matter what. And I think we did a good job proving that to him that day.

There was no manual for me to read about how to deal with this. On second thought, I guess there might have been, but that's not how I deal with situations. I face it right then and there.

I think I ended our conversation with, "So, what else is new with you?" Later, I thought that really was a dumb thing to say.

A few days later, Ron and I were in the car. I was in the middle of a sentence and he hushed me and turned up the volume on the radio. The song played all the way through, and I looked at Ron and both of our eyes were filled with tears.

He had me buy it for Robert to send to him immediately. The

title was "A Father's Love," by George Strait. The main idea of the song is, "Daddies don't just love their children every now and then. It's a love without end."

Now that was a tearjerker. I think it even touched Berto.

CHAPTER FIVE
The Abercrombie Syndrome

The belief among gay men that wearing clothing from Abercrombie & Fitch will make them as sexy as the men in the Abercrombie ads

One of the things that I love most about New York is its variety—variety in theater, restaurants, nightclubs, neighborhoods, and what I was presently most concerned with: men. An eligible gay man could choose the muscled-up Chelsea clone or a skinny, tattooed hottie from the East Village. He could go to Hell's Kitchen for a younger businessman, the Upper East Side for the Connecticut Wall Street type, or the Upper West Side for the WASPs who think they are living on the edge just being there. Yet no matter how big the variety is in New York, one thing remains utterly consistent in the gay community: the obsession over the perfect body, i.e., no fat. Every gay bar, nightclub, and gym is filled with them. Huge biceps, amazing bubble butts, perfectly chiseled abs, and huge pecs—all of which I didn't have.

As a true product of the Midwest, my biggest workout was driving to the liquor store and carrying the keg into a truck. I honestly don't think I heard the word "abs" until I moved to New York. Sure, there were guys with great bodies at my college, but they were on our sports teams, and I thought they were *born* that way.

Yet, everywhere I turned in New York, there were these beautiful men either selling gym memberships, partying at the hottest nightclubs, or sometimes just skipping the pretense and selling the sex itself. I was definitely ripe for buying into the fantasy of what it meant to be gay in New York. If I could obtain "the look" of these men, I'd have this ready-made life complete with friends and places to hang out, dance, and eat. This was a world that was the equivalent of gay fast food to me, and like every good Midwesterner, that was my cuisine of choice.

My mom's fear of me ending up alone weighed heavily on my mind, and if I didn't want to be some crazy whose only loves were his computer and Madonna CD collection, I realized I needed to get to a gym and fast. However, my Antonio Sabato Jr. body had to be put on layaway, because I was scheduled to make a trip home to visit my parents. It was my first "outing" home.

I stepped off the plane feeling a sense of empowerment. I was honest and open about who I was. I was a New Yorker now. Who cared that I'd been living in New York for less than a year? I was already cooler. I knew about things before the rest of the world. And even if I didn't have the shredded body of my peers in New York, I still had a better physique than ninety percent of Bloomington. I was definitely "feeling myself," so to speak.

My first few days home, I did nothing but sleep. I'd been living in the city that never slept and I needed some rest. Finally, after I came out of a groggy stupor, I made my way to the kitchen, where I found my mother, purse in hand, ready to go.

"Are you ready?" she asked.

"For?" I said, grabbing a chocolate chip cookie from the pantry.

"I want you to come to a Weight Watchers meeting with me. I talk about you all the time in our group, and I'd love for the girls to meet you."

"Girls? Group? Is this Weight Watchers or AA?" I replied. She stared at me for a second and then went to the garage. Within seconds, I was sitting next to her in the car.

We sat in the near-empty parking lot at seven in the morning waiting for her group leader, Diane, to arrive. It felt like going to my first gay bar. I wore dark sunglasses and a New York Yankees cap pulled down over my face, slurped on my espresso, and prayed no one would recognize my mom's car. I stared out the window watching the door. I must have been crazy to come here. What if anyone saw me? A lot of people I went to college with still lived in town. What if they happened to be driving to work and saw me going into a Weight Watchers meeting? What if I was mistaken for an . . . *overeater*? Could I be outed as a Weight Watcher when I wasn't even a member?

I was willing to risk it all to support my mom, or at least that's what I told myself. Anyway, I knew I had to make some sort of change to start getting some attention in Manhattan. So I thought maybe I could pick up some tips without actually having to be "one of them."

Finally, Diane arrived and opened the door for the "early birds," as she called them during the meeting. Oh, God, this was so humiliating. I felt like one of those people who went to the mall at 6 A.M. to exercise.

I followed my mom inside. Just look at the ground, I thought to myself. Don't make eye contact or they'll think you're one of them. My mom went to the desk and they handed her an index card that they record your weight on. She then walked to the middle of the room and began setting up chairs with the other ladies.

"Is this what your meetings are like?" she said, setting a chair down.

"Meetings?" I asked, lining up her chair with the rest.

"Well, I assumed your *group* had meetings. I guess not. Who knew gay men were so unorganized?" she said, smirking.

She thought she was hysterical. I was speechless.

She took her place in line for the scale and I quickly went to find a chair in the back before the meeting began. But before I could sit, the over-the-top, perky Diane stopped me.

"Oh, no you don't," she said sternly. What? I was just sitting. It's not like I took out a Snickers bar.

"I'm sorry?" I said blankly.

"And who are you? You have to be weighed," she said, to my horror.

"Oh no, I don't . . . I'm just . . . well . . . I'm Robert!"

"Great, Robert, come step on the scale for me!"

"Actually, I'm just here to support my mother," I explained.

"Really? Come on, everyone can afford to lose a few pounds," she said, grabbing my waist. (This was the area I referred to as the "troubled area.") I was mortified. I felt like the fat kid all over again, and I was by far the thinnest one there.

She nudged me. "Come on. Don't be shy. We're all a lil' chubby." Oh no she didn't.

She put her arm around my shoulder and led me over to the scale, where Nancy, a woman in her sixties, stood smiling. Oh God, no! I frantically looked around for Mom. She was in deep conversation with another member, who, I realized after looking closer, happened to be my elementary school teacher, Ms. Karen. I sunk my head, hoping she wouldn't notice.

"Just step right up here," Nancy said, smiling.

I reluctantly stood on the scale as she slid the markers to the right.

"Looks like 185," she said enthusiastically.

"One eighty-five?" I said, horrified. If at five foot eleven I was 185 pounds of solid muscle, I'd have been thrilled, but it wasn't muscle.

"Let me take my shoes off," I insisted.

"Sure," she said, her tone changed. She was skeptical. "We got a 'shoebie,' ladies." Everyone, including my mother, sighed. I learned during the car ride home that a "shoebie" was a person who believed removing her shoes made a significant difference when stepping on the scale.

I put my sneakers to the side, stood back on the scale, and took a deep breath.

"One eighty-three and a quarter," she said. I was hoping my shoes weighed a good twenty pounds. Unfortunately, they were more like two.

"Take this card and go join the others," she said.

"Thank you," I said sarcastically. I wanted to gouge out sweet Nancy's eyes. I took a seat next to my mother and counted the minutes until this nightmare ended.

"Welcome, everyone," Diane said enthusiastically. "We have a new member joining us today all the way from New York City, here with his mom, Jane. Everyone, meet Robert!"

A resounding "Hi, Robert" came from the group.

The cheering was confirmation for me, not affirmation. It confirmed that there was, in fact, a hell and that I was in it. I looked around the room and saw another familiar face. It was the mother of a guy I went to school with. I could hear the phone conversation now. "You'll never guess who I saw at Weight Watchers this morning, Kyle. Robert Rave. He was with his mother, and he's not only chubby, but he's gay!"

Just when things couldn't get any worse, I heard Diane say, "Robert, could you get up and say a few things about yourself." My mother looked horrified, but I wasn't certain if it was for me or if she was afraid I'd embarrass her in front of her new friends. She glared at Diane.

"Diane, I don't think he really wants to," she said in my defense.

"Now, Jane, you know part of the process is recognizing why you are here," she continued.

"But Diane, if he doesn't want to," my mother tried to interrupt.

"It's okay, Mom. I'll do it," I said, surprising myself. At that moment, I realized that my mother's love definitely hadn't changed. She was still trying to protect me from embarrassing situations. Then I realized that my being here had nothing to do with trying to reestablish a connection with her, because I had never truly lost it. My role at this meeting was to support her. My being gay was secondary to all other things.

I stood up slowly. "My name is Robert Rave, and I came here today to support my mother, as she's stood by my side her entire life. Now it's my turn to be with her through her struggle with food," I said. I could see some of the ladies tearing up. "I now live in New York City, the land of the beautiful people, and I'm having some issues of my own with body image, so I guess once again my mother was doing me a favor without even realizing it by bringing me here. But then again, that's *my* mom for you—she knows just what I need before I do."

I sat back down and my mom squeezed my arm, and then we listened to the rest of the ladies give their weekly report. A few minutes later, we snuck out while Diane was giving her motivational talk. We went straight to IHOP for a stack of pancakes to celebrate.

Mama Says

When Robert came home that weekend, I told him that since he was finding out who he was, I was going to do some finding out about me. I am sure he thought I meant I was going to find out why he was gay, where it originated, blah, blah. Sorry, Berto, I truly meant only me. Reluctantly, he agreed to go to a Weight Watchers meeting—just to humor me, I think.

He's gay and I'm chubby. He probably figured he could handle meeting my chubby friends if I could handle him being gay.

My first meeting at Weight Watchers was hard. It was embarrassing to walk through those doors. The first person I saw was the mother of one of Robert's classmates in school. She was a real know-it-all. I had a choice. I could either go home and feel sorry for myself and eat snickerdoodles, or I could walk into that meeting and start fresh. I said, *Screw it. You can do this*, and I did.

As the weeks went on, I got to know Diane, the group leader. She was a great girl, about my daughter's age and with a great sense of humor. She didn't care how we looked. Hearing about her struggles with weight made us laugh and sometimes even cry, as we all fought the same battle.

Outside of my Weight Watchers friends, Robert's probably the only person I know other than myself who understands how hard it is to look good and have a good body. He talks a lot about the obsession that gay guys have with the perfect body. He told me that if you didn't meet a certain physical standard, you didn't cut it in the gay community. To me, they sounded like a bunch of catty women. But for that matter, I still feel there is a lot of pressure on women to have a great body, no matter what their age. I have succumbed to it, I think.

However, I have a wonderful husband who sees me as a seventeen-year-old, 110-pound girl who hasn't aged a day since high school. He doesn't see what *I* see when I look in the mirror. Ron says I look great and it just doesn't matter to him. Most women would die to hear this from their husbands. Yet, in a way, it ends up being more destructive, because I kind of feel like he's right, so I don't worry about it and continue to eat what I've been eating and not feel comfortable in my own skin. The bottom line: I wasn't happy with my body, but everybody's got issues—even skinny people have things they don't like about themselves, and for that matter so do gay people. So I guess we're all screwed, huh?

I never imagined that at my age I would be planning my days around Weight Watchers meetings. When I was young, I was a popular person in school and did all the things that most teenage girls did back then. I was a cheerleader, homecoming queen, band member—pretty much any extracurricular activity, I was in it. I loved the outdoors, I loved swimming, I loved waterskiing—frankly, I just loved life. I wanted to sing and dance and enjoy every moment.

As I got older I let my weight control me instead of me controlling it, and eventually I had to give up so many of the things I loved to do.

Little did I know when I joined Weight Watchers and started losing weight that everyone else in the family would decide they also needed to lose weight. We are a close family, and I was happy that they wanted to lose weight. I soon became the keeper of the points for everyone.

I know Robert went that morning to support me, but he left that meeting realizing it would help him, too. So together, we began facing the same demons.

He was reaching out for help to look good so he could find a life partner. And me? I was just trying to find the person inside me, the one who loved life.

CHAPTER SIX

To Wax or Not to Wax

The long-running argument between my mother and
me on whether a man should wax

M y mother called me that morning to let me know she had a new
recipe for jerk chicken, a mere three points a serving. Who needed
fancy Manhattan brunches when I had my mother calling me about
jerk chicken? Unfortunately (or fortunately, depending on whom
you ask), I didn't have time to jot it down as I was running late for
an appointment.

"What kind of appointment?" she asked.

"It's personal," I explained.

"Oh, God! Is everything all right?" she asked, sounding irritated.
I blamed her irritability on getting up at five every morning, while
she blamed it on my father.

"Everything's fine."

"If it's fine, what's the appointment for? Oh, God! Is it your health?
You're okay, aren't you? You've been practicing safe sex? For God's
sake, what is it?"

I was even more nervous about this than when I told her I was
gay.

"I'm going for a wax."

"You're what?!"

"I'm going for a wax."

Her panic turned to laughter. "That's a good one, Berto." (She
loved to call me by this name when making jokes. Clearly she shared
my taste for all things Latin.) After spending several minutes convinc-
ing her I was deadly serious, she told me she didn't understand why

any man would want to wax. In her opinion, "Men don't do that sort of thing, only women."

I knew when I came out of the closet that I would have to educate my family on a lot of aspects of being gay, but somehow this was all too much for me. What would next week's conversation be? The Joys of Gay Sex?

I continued to rush her off the phone before she asked the dreaded question that I knew was coming next. I didn't need my mother to know *that*. But she was going in *that* direction. I quickly tried to deflect.

"How's Gram's knee?" I asked, semi-concerned. (She had just had excruciating knee surgery the week before.)

"She'll live. Now, what the hell is this sicko going to wax?"

There it was. Right before me. A question most gay men don't even like talking about with their closest friends, even though they know everyone's been down that road. "If you must know, my chest, stomach, and back."

"You have a hairy back?" she said with disgust.

"No, but I don't even like having a little bit there."

"That's so gay," she said. "Sorry, you know what I mean." She had nothing to be sorry about—it was so gay even *I* was more than embarrassed to be doing it, let alone having a conversation about it with my mother. Remember, this is before the word "manscaping" became part of our lexicon thanks to *Queer Eye for the Straight Guy*.

To my great fortune, my sister, her husband, and their two kids happened to be visiting my parents that weekend.

"Hold on. Julie just walked in," she said. I could hear her muffling the phone, but in the way only a mother could, meaning I heard every word. "Your brother is getting waxed!" she said, distraught.

I could hear my sister in the background. "Really? Maybe Jeff should do it. He's hairy." Jeff, my brother-in-law, is a great guy, a family man, a man's man, but not someone with whom I want to share my personal grooming habits.

"Jeff, come in here for a minute," I heard my sister yell. This was not happening to me.

"Ma, I gotta go. I'm going to be late for Rima," I said.

"Rima? This person has a name? What kind of person aspires to pull body hair off someone's most intimate areas? More importantly, what kind of person *lets* her do it?"

"Actually, she is about your age, and she's this great *normal* Russian woman who tells me all about her daughter studying classical piano and her son who just finished his sophomore year of high school." (I left out that this was usually when I was lying face down while she was ripping hot wax off my ass.)

"Oh, my God! I just can't even . . ."

At that moment, my brother-in-law walked into the room, and I heard my sister telling him to raise his shirt. He sounded confused but did as he was told, as he knew better than to not follow orders when my mom and sister were in the room.

"Yeah, you could definitely use a wax. It's like a sweater," I heard my sister say. "I can take you to my lady at home. She's quick and painless." I could hear my mother's groans.

"I really have to go now. I'm going to be late."

"One second. Your dad just walked in from the office," she said.
Great.

"Why is Jeff standing there with his shirt lifted? I don't need to see that shit," I heard him say. I love my dad! He nailed exactly what I was thinking.

"Do you know what your son is doing? He's getting waxed," my mom said. "He's having his hair on his chest, back, and God knows where else ripped off with hot wax," she barked.

"I don't really see the big deal, Jane," he said, to my surprise.

"What?" my mother and I said in sync.

"It's really no different than our backyard," he said. "When we first moved in, the trees in the back were totally overgrown and the bushes looked like they hadn't been trimmed in years. You said yourself it looked like a vacant lot. We didn't even want to invite anyone over to spend time in the backyard until we cleaned it up," he continued.

"Where are you going with this?" she asked.

"I'm saying Robert needs to trim his tree and bush before anyone spends time in his backyard."

Mama Says

I was eleven years old when I first discovered my dad's shaving kit in my parents' bathroom. At school a couple of my friends commented on my legs, which were fairly hairy for an eleven-year-old. But I was blond so it was barely visible. I never really thought about getting rid of the hair on my legs until that moment. It was fate and I just happened to be in the bathroom with the right tools to complete the job.

I sat on my dad's shelf and stretched out my left leg and smeared cream all over it. I grabbed his straight razor and slowly moved up my leg. It wasn't so bad, I thought. I did another row and another until the shaving cream was completely gone. I looked at myself in the mirror and smiled. I felt like an adult. That is, until I looked down and saw my bloody leg. I opened the medicine cabinet and began applying Band-Aids, when I heard my mother knocking on the bathroom door.

"What are you doing in there?" she asked.

"Um, nothing?" I said.

My mother knew me better than anyone else and quickly demanded I come out.

"Fine," I said, and plopped down off the shelf, opened the bathroom door, and took a few steps out into the hallway.

"What was going on in there?" my mother asked.

"Nothing," I said. I hoped she hadn't noticed the multiple lacerations on my legs.

"Looks like something to me. You're bleeding," she said. I thought my eight Band-Aids had covered any sign of blood.

"Oh," I said and stared at my mother with wide eyes. I wasn't exactly sure what my next move should be. I decided to appeal to her as a fellow woman. "Patti Carlson started shaving her legs and I thought it was time."

"You could have seriously hurt yourself!" my mom scolded. "You better hope your father doesn't notice that you messed with his shaving kit." My mom was the calmer one, whereas my dad was the strict disciplinarian.

I wasn't sure what the appropriate decision was in this situation. I could either feign crying to escape a hard punishment or just stand my ground, but before I could get a word out my mother bent over to inspect my leg.

Suddenly, she got very quiet. I wasn't sure if she was going to smack me or send me to my room. "Well, you better get in there and do the other leg. You don't want to look like a crazy person," she said, as if I didn't already look like I'd escaped from the psych ward with my bandage-covered legs. Forget that I was eleven and using a straight razor, more importantly I was to make sure I didn't have one hairy ape leg.

"Okay," I said and darted into the bathroom before she could say another word.

The second leg went much smoother than the first. I needed only three bandages. I considered this a major accomplishment.

Without my dad's knowledge, I continued to practice for several months and by the time I got into junior high I had the best-shaved legs in my entire class. As for waxing, that is a different story. I've never done it and I probably won't. Actually, if I did, I wouldn't tell anyone.

Now that I know a little about gay men, I just don't get why they feel they have to wax every hair on their body. Do they like pain?

Do all gay people—men and women—wax? Believe me, I am learning as I go along. I'm trying here.

I personally think some chest hair is attractive. I don't know why Ron doesn't have any. My son-in-law should wax, though, since he has a lot of body hair. I discovered it one day in the kitchen. I guess when I think about it, who wants to be with someone who feels like he's wearing a sweater?

Bottom line, my son waxes—I have even dropped him off at a waxing salon—and while we're on the subject, he has better manicured nails than I do. And there is nothing feminine about him. I'd like to be more like my son. He is getting it all together. Maybe I should start going with him, although I suspect that might just send him over the edge. I would like to meet this Rima, though, and find out why the hell she does what she does.

CHAPTER SEVEN
Point-if-ication

To have been brainwashed into counting everything you eat and putting it into a point system so you can systematically drive your friends, family, and neighbors insane. The (un)rave: a less-than-enthusiastic view of the author by every available gay man; no calories, no taste, no fun.

I was returning to New York after another chaotic trip to visit my parents when, during my flight home, I pulled out a packet of Weight Watchers material that my mother had given me after we attended another meeting together. I quickly covered it up, as if I were reading porn. I looked at my chart. It was very official, like some sort of medical record. It had my name, address, social security number, and of course my weight, 184, in huge letters at the bottom.

I pulled two thick paperback books out from the vinyl folder. If the lady sitting to my right had any question about my sexuality, she quickly got her answer. Not only did I have a vinyl folder, but a vinyl folder with diet materials enclosed. Gay, gay, gay!

Book Number One was the *Complete Food Companion*, a list of every possible type of food you could ever eat—everything from Jamaican store-bought coffee to Oscar Mayer cheese dogs—each one, of course, containing a numeric value. Two hundred and fifty pages worth, to be exact. I immediately placed Book Number Two in the seat pocket in front of me for the next weight-challenged traveler, because for a New Yorker, Book Number Two was useless. It was called the *Dining Out Companion: Point Values for Food Served at 57 Popular Chain Restaurants*. Apparently, the folks at Weight Watchers weren't *city* friendly, because if they had been, they'd know that I'd be breaking a fundamental law on several fronts.

It's an unwritten rule as a hip, young New Yorker that you *never* eat at a chain restaurant. Furthermore, as a *gay* New Yorker, when you think "dining experiences," you think T.G.I. Hooligans. Eating at a chain was not only frowned upon because it was so gauche, but also because much of the food is fried, and fried equals fat to Manhattan gay boys.

The flight attendant sashayed down the aisle with her beverage cart and snacks in hand. I was armed and ready to put Weight Watchers to its first test. She handed me a Diet Coke (my personal version of crack cocaine) and a snack pack that included the following: one Life Savers Creme Saver, two crackers, a two-pack of Oreo cookies, and some sort of processed cheese.

I went straight for the Oreos, but before I devoured them, I looked it up in the book. Five points for two cookies. Doesn't sound bad. The crackers were three, the cheese was four, and the piece of candy I didn't count, because I didn't consider candy to be food. Twelve points! That didn't seem so bad. I remembered reading that thirty points was reasonable for a meal. I had eighteen to spare. As I tallied up the points, the woman to my right leaned over and said, "You forgot the Creme Saver."

"Oh, no. It's not really food," I explained. "It's candy."

"Look, I've been on the points for the last nine months, and it counts!" she said with a note of irritability.

"So what is it?" I asked.

"Two points."

"Okay, that's not so bad."

"Fourteen points for a snack?" she barked. "You're only allowed thirty per *day*."

Oh shit. I sat in silence for the remainder of the flight.

I arrived back at my apartment feeling even more self-aware. I had an arsenal of Weight Watcher materials, including the essential "Points Finder," the sliding scale used to calculate the point value of anything you put into your mouth. (Insert sexual innuendo here.)

Personally, I believe the use of the word "point" was a clever way of disguising the real word they wanted to use, *pontificate*, another word for "preach" or "teach dogma." The last thing I needed was some weight-loss program preaching to me. I had enough pressure trying to exist in this big gay world.

I was elated about one thing: If I exercised, I would receive bonus points that I could use to eat something of my choice, depending on how many points I worked off. I had belonged to the gym, but until this point it was more for social reasons than to actually work out. I was new to the city and wanted to meet people. Now I had *reason* to use the machines.

Later that day, I arrived at the gym determined to earn extra food points. I had just finished doing bench presses, and as I walked to the drinking fountain, I felt my face begin to burn. He was one of the most beautiful men I'd ever seen. Six feet tall, with jet-black hair, thick eyebrows, and piercing brown eyes, he was amazing. As he smiled at a friend, I saw the dimple on his cheek. And his body? Flawless. Not an ounce of fat. He was muscular but not meathead big. For a second, I actually thought I had worked out too hard and was hallucinating. He was all man, not one thing feminine about him. He was a hybrid of everything I'd always fantasized about.

And he looked right through me when he passed.

However, that night a magical moment happened, in the form of a phone call from my mother. "I'm so excited. I just got the best recipe for a chocolate pie that is only two points per slice," she gushed.

"What's in it?" I said sadly.

"Uh-oh. What's the matter with you?"

"It's nothing you would understand."

"Why's that?"

"Because . . ."

"Well?"

"Because it has to do with a guy I like," I said. There was a long silence, and I wasn't sure if she was lying on the floor having a heart attack.

To my surprise, she said, "Well, it's his loss. Screw him. There're other guys."

Suddenly, I was the one who felt like I should be on the floor with heart failure. I took a deep breath, exhaled, and said, "So, tell me about this recipe. I need a good dessert. I'm starving." From that day on, my mother and I never missed our daily phone call, our time to talk about "the points" . . . and men.

Weeks later, thanks to my mother and the neurotic Diane from Weight Watchers calling to track my progress, I had lost around eight pounds. But it didn't matter; I still wasn't getting the results I wanted. People barely spoke to me at the gym even with my new lighter self. Hell, I had even paid $150 for blond highlights to make me even more appealing. (Could you get any gayer?) I'd had enough. I was sick of watching every last thing I ate, not to mention journaling it every goddamn second of the day. I was point obsessed. Like my diet, my life had become strictly regimented, and I was in drastic need of a change.

My mom called me after Weight Watchers to chart her latest loss with me. She was kicking ass, but as only she can do, she could tell in my voice that once again something was amiss.

"Oh, God. Now what?" she said, interrupting my congratulatory speech.

"What do you mean?" I asked.

"I know you, so you might as well tell me and get it over with."

"It's nothing . . . okay, fine. I just thought that once I started to lose some weight, maybe I'd get asked out—hell, at this point, I'd be happy to get a second glance," I said solemnly.

She sighed. "Well, this is what we were afraid of when you told us you were gay."

"What?"

"Being *alone*." As she said it, I felt the word "alone" resonate. I could tell by her voice that she felt awful for me, but then her tone quickly changed.

"I saw this article about a book called *Finding the Boyfriend Within* in one of my magazines. I think you should buy it. The summary sounds exactly like what you are going through."

"What?" I said angrily. "You were reading a magazine for women!"

"Oh, calm down, the book is for gay men. Give it a shot. You might like it. Besides, the guy on the cover is handsome. I have to run to get your dad some Preparation H before Kroger's closes, but go buy it."

For God's sake, I was at an age where I needed to find the boyfriend on the corner, *not* within. Wait a second . . . did she say she needed to buy Preparation H? Anyway, there was no way, no how that I was buying that damn book (although she did say the author was cute). Nope, hell would freeze over before I bought such a completely ridiculous book.

Well, the first chapter of *Finding the Boyfriend Within*—yes, apparently hell did freeze over—goes into great detail about the author, this successful gay man in his mid-forties. He was at a dinner party one night where some obnoxious, bitter queen was asking him a million questions about his frequent appearance in the gossip columns. When the question turned to relationships, the jaded queen in question said, "What's it all worth if none of it has gotten you a boyfriend?" The author responded that he was dating "the boyfriend within," to the snarls of the jaded queen. Normally, I would be the jaded one in this story, because honestly, if someone said they were working on the boyfriend within, I'd probably burst out into laughter.

The first exercise of the book dealt with working on your guiding voice within. Apparently we all have one; we just ignore it. My mother always taught me that the voices in my head were not a good thing, so I turned the volume way down.

To begin the procedure, I was instructed to sit at a table with a "tablet of paper and two felt-tip pens." This was problem number one for me. A tablet of paper and two felt-tip pens? Was this 1982? I quickly flipped to the front of the book to see when the book had been printed. Nope. It was definitely the nineties.

I took a deep breath and thought, what the hell? My own mother already thought I needed to get my mental house in order, so I might as well give it a go. I turned on my computer and was ready for magic.

The following is my first Q&A:

ME: Hello.

VOICE: Hello.

ME: You're nuts. They are going to check us into a crazy house soon.

VOICE: No they're not. We're fine.

ME: I'm sitting here having a dialogue with myself and referring to myself in the third person. Who do I think I am, Whitney Houston?

VOICE: Cut the shit.

ME: What?

VOICE: The sarcasm.

ME: Whoa. What's happening here?

VOICE: Quit trying to be funny and witty. You're obviously here for a reason. Now let's get to it.

ME: Hey, Bossy McBoss, don't tell me why I'm here.

VOICE: I'm leaving.

ME: Fine! Wait. I have questions.

VOICE: (silence)

ME: Come on.

VOICE: (silence)

ME: *Please!* I want to talk and figure this shit out.

VOICE: Okay, but no more bullshit—if you start up, I'm gone.

ME: Only I would have a passive-aggressive inner voice.

VOICE: You were saying?

ME: Nothing. It's not important. Okay, here goes my first question. What's wrong with me?

VOICE: Nothing. You're fine.

ME: Then why won't anyone pay any attention to me—or even feign momentary interest?

VOICE: What do you expect when you look at the ground every time somebody walks by?

ME: But I don't do that.

VOICE: I'm your inner voice. I know these things, hello?

ME: But why?

VOICE: Because you feel like you are not good enough or cute enough to warrant their attention.

ME: Maybe.

VOICE: You use your weight and your physical appearance as a reason for not opening yourself to others. You feel less than—

ME: Whoa, whoa, whoa. Calm down. I didn't ask for all of this.

VOICE: Yes, you did, whether you realize it or not.

ME: But why do I even give a rat's ass about any of this? I mean, none of this should matter in the grand scheme of life. I'm a nice person—and for the most part, a good person. I try to do right by people the best I can.

VOICE: You could have more friends if you wanted, but you feel that they'll eventually leave because you're not good enough, so you save yourself the pain of their loss and keep only a few.

ME: (silence)

VOICE: Are we done here?

ME: (silence)

VOICE: Go ahead. Ask it. I know what you're thinking, remember?

ME: But why does any of this matter to me at all? Logic tells me *it really shouldn't!*

VOICE: Because you're scared.

ME: Of?

VOICE: Of being alone.

I turned off the computer as if it had become possessed. Maybe this book wasn't such a joke after all. Maybe I did want to find somebody for more than five minutes, but maybe I needed to figure out my own shit first. Or maybe I was ready for Rolling Meadows Mental Home.

Mama Says

When I look back on my younger days, I realize I didn't personally know any gay people. I would hear my parents talk about "so and so" and how a certain "someone" in town lived with another man. When that happened, it was the talk of the town.

You have to understand, I come from a community of 1,400 people. I grew up in a town where black men had to be out of town by sundown. No wonder people didn't want to come out of the closet. If a person was even suspected of being gay, the other men would make his life a living hell.

I didn't like anyone being made fun of, whether that person was in the closet, fat, or ugly. We are all a little odd when it comes right down to it, but we still for the most part do a lot of the same things. The only big difference I can see in gay people is that heterosexual people are way too interested in what gay people do in their bedroom. I don't give a rat's you-know-what who does what in their bedroom. In my opinion, the people who do probably don't even have a sex life. Being gay, as my son tells me, doesn't mean you just have sex all the time.

I had a friend in school who was adopted from "the Islands," whatever that means. He had some color, he wasn't considered either black or white, and he was always called "sissy." He had a tough time. His parents were quite a bit older than most; they were very strict and didn't understand all the torment he went through at school. I don't know how he survived. He was teased and taunted all day long, and then he went to a home where he got into trouble for looking at his parents the wrong way.

These were the first things I thought about when Robert told us he was gay. I think about that boy when I think of what my son will have to go through. People can be mean, and I don't want that for my son. He is such a happy person—he always has been. I don't want to see his spirit fade just because he's gay. He is the joy of my husband's life and mine, but we can't protect him from a bunch of jerks. He's an adult, but I'm still his mom.

Finding the Boyfriend Within seemed like a good resource for him. He'd been complaining about feeling alone. Instantly going into mom mode, I found out about the book in a magazine and suggested he pick it up. I know I could use a book like that—not because I need to find a boyfriend, just because we all could use a little self-understanding.

I think I'll ask to borrow his copy.

PART TWO:

Changing Weather

CHAPTER EIGHT
The Forecast

Doppler radar shows a cold front moving toward
New York City by way of Bloomington

The planets had been in some serious misalignment lately. Weird things were happening all around me. People began to look me in the eyes on the streets. I could've sworn I got a "What's up?" from the hot guy from the gym. Perhaps *sunny days* were in my future. But like every other weather pattern, it was only temporary.

During the winter, I'd been told about a magical place for gays and lesbians. A place where there were no cars, just miles of endless beach. A place where hordes of beautiful gay men were pulling their groceries in a red wagon to and from their beach houses. A place where successful and sophisticated men rented houses together for the summer and celebrated a real sense of community. It was like nothing I had ever heard about growing up, but then again I hadn't heard of any gay people growing up, except for Father Gene, who liked his "hot toddies." Unfortunately, no one in my school district knew he was talking about one hot toddy in particular, Todd Koening, our school's quarterback.

Eager to sign up and join a friend in his "share house," I knew I'd have to go to my parents for the cash. My salary from my theater PR job didn't cover my rent, let alone some glamour house out in the "Pines," as they're called.

"What the hell is Fire Island?" my mother said. I made the sales pitch to her, telling her how it was essential to my mental health that I spend my weekends there, as I couldn't spend one more weekend bored and alone in the city. "But you've never even seen this place." It was a sincere question, and not meant to be an attack.

Oh, she was good, but I was ready for anything. "It's right on the beach," I argued, sounding more like fifteen than twenty-one. I had used similar bargaining tactics when negotiating for an expensive Ralph Lauren sweater that I swore I'd wear at every major family function. She had given in then. I bought the sweater and wore it one time to Christmas dinner. It made me itch, and the sweater mysteriously disappeared from my closet, never to be heard from again.

"Thirty-five hundred is a lot for two weekends a month," she said, once again quite logically. I wasn't having it. Luckily for me, it was the age of the Internet, and as we were speaking I did a search on the computer. Unfortunately, this was before DSL, so I'd have to stall.

"Have you seen anyone I went to school with?" I knew this would take up the required amount of time for me to find the key words I needed to seal my real estate transaction.

"Actually, I ran into Mary Whitmore." Mary Whitmore was the mother of one of my former best friends in high school, Richard. She was a busybody and had to be the "cool mom" to everyone. I never thought she was. I viewed her more as a woman in denial.

"How's Richard doing?" I really didn't care, but the only thing that was coming up from my search was all the porn titles with the name Fire Island in them. I didn't think they would help my case.

"He's just gotten married and is expecting his first," my mother said.

"Oh, that's great. I always thought he was gay," I said. I expected her to laugh, but she didn't. "Hello? I realize I may not be Eddie Murphy, but that was at least funny enough for a snicker. What gives?"

"Mary told me she was so sorry to hear about you," she said dryly.

I immediately peeled my eyes away from the computer screen filled with half-naked men and stared at the floor. "Sorry for me? Why?" I asked, hoping that maybe she had been misinformed and heard that I'd been diagnosed with some terminal disease.

"I asked her the same question," my mother said. "She said she was sorry to hear that you were gay and that I must be just devastated."

I could feel the sting in my eyes and my cheeks burning, and there was a sharp pain in the back of my throat.

"Oh."

Sensing I didn't want to hear any more, she moved on. "I might as well tell you this, too, while we're on the subject."

"Go on," I said.

"The other day, your dad ran into Stan, your ex-college roommate, at the Wesleyan basketball game. He told your father that Joanne Luding at the registrar's office was telling your friends that were still in school that you and your dad weren't getting along because you were a 'homosexual.'"

"What? What a bitch," I yelled into the phone. Not only was it a lie, but it was a cruel one. One thing that I never expected when I came out of the closet was that the people I loved would be treated differently because of me. It was a mean thing to say to anyone, especially a parent.

"Your dad's reaction was the same as yours. He told Stan that Joanne is a fucking bitch who should be fired. He's actually going to his friend, the dean of students over there, to fuck her up and tell her not to mess with our family."

That's one thing about my family. We're the nicest people in the world, but you mess with us once and we get all Sopranos on you.

"And what happened with Mary?" I asked.

"I told her not to feel sorry for me because you had a boyfriend who was beautiful and rich, which is more than she could say for that fat, balding husband of hers. So as much as we appreciate her 'sorrow,' she really should keep it for herself and her own family problems, including *her own* closeted gay son."

I tried my best to come up with a fake laugh. It was funny as hell, but I was still so bothered that people would be that ignorant to my parents. I felt violated. Disgusted. It was all I could do to avoid having a breakdown on the phone.

"So, do you have those names yet?" my mom asked.

"What?" I said, still in a daze.

"Well, I assumed you were trying to find out some key words to get me to buy into this Fire Island thing, so give it to me."

I hadn't had so much luck, just a few pseudo-celebrities who had been there. "Calvin Klein and Michael Kors are there all the time," I said, knowing she'd recognize the names. "It could be good for my career," I added.

She laughed. "Only if you slept with them. And *don't* do that," she barked.

Several budgetary promises later, my parents finally agreed to lend me the money.

Two weeks prior to the beginning of summer, my friend Lance, who asked me to join his share house in the first place, now informed me that his house was full since one of the guys was bringing his Venezuelan boyfriend in for the summer. Instead of calling immigration on Mr. Venezuela so I could regain my place in the house, I took Lance's suggestion to share a house with some friend of a friend of a friend. Ah, the joys of not being particularly popular (or Latin).

I thought about bailing on the house altogether, but my parents had already sent the check, and buying a new summer wardrobe with the money would definitely not have gone over so well.

I packed my bags, took the train from Manhattan to Long

Island, and arrived to see the ferries approach the loading zone. Meanwhile, another group of fairies were getting loaded at a small dockside bar as they waited to board. I took it all in with a mixture of excitement and fear. Following hordes of men onto the boat, I felt like I was on a floating nightclub. As we pulled away from the shore and I looked back at Long Island, I felt a great sense of relief and relaxation. I wasn't worried about how I was going to pay my rent, and I'd forgotten about the Mary Whitmores of the world.

Fifteen minutes later, I arrived at a very cute house right on the beach, occupied by a group of men I had never met and didn't know a thing about. The youngest was sixteen years my senior. Besides myself, there were six other "housemates" inhabiting the summer house at 404 Ocean Drive. The "gays" called the house quaint and charming. Being from a small town in Illinois, I called it small and dirty. I don't think the house had gone through a renovation since the early '70s. I'd never seen so many different shades of brown. There were three bedrooms for six guys. I suddenly felt like I was on an episode of the gay version of *The Real World*. I was the last to arrive.

"Steven! The masseuse is here!" a buff man in his early forties said as he walked into the kitchen with a margarita. Every stereotype I'd heard about gay men growing up was suddenly prancing before me, in Speedos no less.

"Oh, I'm not the masseuse, but I'm flattered," I joked.

"Houseboy?"

"No," I said. "Keep trying?"

"Drug dealer?"

"Definitely not."

"Well, if you aren't one of the three, you are of no use to me," he said. He went back to his room and shut the door.

"You must be Robert," a warm voice said from behind me.

"Yes, that's me," I said nervously.

"I'm Corey. Welcome to Fire Island."

"Margaritas and foie gras, anyone?" Jeremy, a very masculine-looking (but definitely not masculine-sounding) man with a Long Island accent walked out from another room with a platter in hand. I hadn't even put my bags away and I was already going through initiation. And I thought *my* fraternity was bad!

"What is he *on*?" said a hushed voice from the kitchen. His name was Fred, and he appeared to be the sane one of the group. I came to this conclusion due to his smart eyewear.

I thought Fred was being too hard on our gracious host, but then again Jeremy did seem happy, like Jack Nicholson in *The Shining* happy.

"Probably a little Zoloft," I said innocently.

"What? What is that? Is that some kind of new street drug? Are you one of those druggie party boys?" Fred said in rapid fire.

"No, it's a prescription drug, and if I was some druggie party boy, do you think I'd be standing here?" I said.

"Good, I don't do drugs or bugs," he said. I gravitated toward the margaritas. I had a feeling it was going to be a long night.

Maybe it was the difference in age, but I'd always imagined a "share house" being exactly that. You rent a room in a beach house, you come and go as you please, you buy your own food, you hang out at the pool or the beach, and you clean up after your own mess. I realized I couldn't have been more wrong when Larry assembled the group around the coffee table to go over the "house rules":

1. Every guest must pay $50 at the beginning of each weekend for groceries.
2. Every guest must pay $50 at the beginning of each weekend for the cleaning lady.
3. Dinner is cooked after "High Tea" at 10:30 P.M.—one crew cooks, and the other cleans.

4. There is to be no loud music after 11 P.M.
5. If you bring home a trick, there is a $50 "guest fee."
6. The entire house will plant flowers and tend to them the first of every month.
7. Our house will be dressing up as The Golden Girls for Dance on the Beach 15.

This was not the free–flowing house that I'd expected. I began thinking of all the nasty things I could do to my friend Lance. Replace his protein shakes with powdered laxatives? Spike his moisturizer with cheap bronzer?

Before I could develop my diabolical plans, I was ushered off to the evening's first activity, High Tea. When everyone kept saying High Tea, I kept imagining British people sitting around sipping Earl Grey out of fancy china. When Corey and I walked into the bar, I quickly realized that High Tea meant that most of the patrons were high from either the drinks or the narcotics. The other explanation was that the boys who thought they were really something had their noses so "high" in the air that they wouldn't look down at you.

This was still only a few months into my Weight Watchers program, but I was feeling good about myself. I was wearing a nice outfit, I had brushed my teeth, and I was wearing some cologne borrowed from one of the guys in the house. Maybe this wouldn't be so bad! Corey and I stood in line for yet another drink and someone behind us said, "Oh, how cute. He has love handles!"

What a complete asshole! I thought. Who says that out loud? Then my second thought was to feel awful for the poor out-of-shape guy who had the love handles. He must not have been dressed appropriately.

"Corey," I heard the voice say. Corey turned around. "Corey, aren't you going to introduce us to your friend with the love handles?" the effeminate man said, even louder. Mortified, I prayed that an ash from some unsuspecting gay's cigarette would land in this man's eye. I hoped that the blender making the frozen margaritas would short and cause an electrical fire, engulfing the entire building in wild flames.

"This is Robert," Corey said. "It's his first summer here, so be nice."

"He's got a lot to learn," the man snickered.

His friend elbowed him in the chest. "Don't mind him. He's had a little too much fun with Tina."

I wasn't privy to who Tina was (crystal meth), but by the end of the summer it seemed as though she had made her rounds through many of the houses in Fire Island. While Corey continued making polite conversation, I retreated to the back of the bar, willing it to be time to go back to the house for dinner. On the off chance that dinner would be delayed, I began looking around the bar for someone to talk to. I didn't want to be the only person standing alone looking and feeling like a complete loser.

For the last twenty-one years I'd had the same MO. When forced to compete on any level, I would walk away. I didn't want anyone knowing my secret interests—that would leave me way too open for attack. Instead, I'd give up and move on to something that I wasn't as interested in. Looking around at the rest of the guys at High Tea, I made a stand. I could either be the wackjob wallflower talking to himself, or I could actually try to talk to someone. Half of these guys were a bunch of girls anyway. All I had to do was yell "boo" and they'd go running to their Prada-covered houses. So I made my move.

I approached a nice Italian-looking guy with dark features named Angelo. He was sexy, with a nice muscular body, and most importantly for me, he was masculine. After talking to him, I found out that he was thirty-one, almost ten years my senior. He was getting better and better as I found out he also had a good, stable job. (Nice dinners out on the town!)

High Tea came and went, and there Angelo and I sat, still talking about everything from music to movies (hey, this was Fire Island, not the Museum of Modern Art). We went to the one restaurant on the island, and I could barely focus on the food. I'm not sure if I was falling for him or if I was just happy that someone was paying attention to me, but either way I wanted to enjoy a summer romance. That night, neither one of us wanted to pay $50 for the other to stay over, so we consummated our romance by the pool of my share house. In retrospect, that should have been red flag number one. Red flag number two should have been that I saw Angelo only every other weekend and never when we both were back in the city. But again I didn't mind; I was just happy to be with someone as cute as him. I didn't think I was capable of getting anything better.

Two months later, on one hot July evening, Corey and I went dancing at the Pavilion, Fire Island's "nightclub." Again, what the gays would call a nightclub, I called a fire trap. Corey and I made our way onto the dance floor and I noticed my Angelo dancing. "He looks great, doesn't he, Corey! He's such a hot dancer." I then got closer and realized that Angelo was dancing with another man; in fact, he was grinding with another man. That man was none other than the girly guy who had insulted my love handles two months prior. Then I saw them both do a bump on the dance floor. This explained a lot about Angelo and his lack of commitment to seeing me. I later found out he often went on three-day binges and would stay holed up in a sex club the entire time.

I went outside to collect myself. I couldn't compete with that. I didn't even want to.

Corey told Angelo what had happened, and he quickly found me. After listening to his profuse apologies, I forgave him and said

I was willing to overlook it, but I told him he should ease up on the drugs. We went to the bar and got a drink. "You're really sexy," he said. No one had ever said that to me, no guy at least. It made me feel so alive.

"Thank you, but you're sexier."

"Oh, I know," he said, straight-faced. "So anyway, what do you think about us?" he said with a huge smile while his eyes darted back and forth.

"What do you mean?"

"You know . . . us? What do you think about our relationship?" he said, still smiling.

"Well . . ." I took a deep breath. "I'm really happy. I'm so glad we've met, and I've really enjoyed getting to know you. I really want to have a future with you. I have to be honest. I think I could fall in love with you," I said, looking deep into his saucer-shaped pupils.

"Really?" he said, surprised.

"Yeah, why?"

"Because I feel nothing for you," he deadpanned. "Not a thing one way or the other. In fact, I'm ambivalent to you."

I think it was the meanest thing anyone could have said to me. I felt I'd been ripped into tiny pieces and then thrown into a bucket of shit. I walked home that night and lay in bed and listened to all of the guys walking to house parties, laughing, enjoying them-selves, calling each other "Mary" or "Girl." I knew I'd never be a part of this group. Maybe *everyone* felt ambivalent toward me. Hell, up until now, I'd felt ambivalent toward me.

I packed my bags the next day and never returned. On the train ride back to Manhattan, I thought about Mary Whitmore and her son, Richard, and Joanne Luding. I wondered if they were right to feel sorry for my parents. I wanted there to be some great answer or some sign of a greater purpose, something to assure me that it was really the Whitmores and Ludings that should have been sorry. But there wasn't. That wasn't the world we lived in. The one thing that I did know was that no matter what, I'd still have both my parents' love and support, so there would be no pity parade for me.

I mysteriously disappeared from Fire Island, never to be heard from again, much like the itchy Ralph Lauren sweater I'd bought with borrowed money as a teenager.

Mama Says

When Robert told his dad and me that he was renting a summer cottage with six other men, I thought, *How lucky is he?* I had always wanted to do that, too. Anyway, that's another book.

After agreeing to lend him the rent, I told everybody I knew that he was renting a cottage on Fire Island. In fact, when I ran into an old neighbor at the grocery store, I bragged to her that Robert had rented a summer house on the beach. When she asked where, I told her with pride, "Fire Island. It's very chic and quaint. They actually use little red wagons to carry their groceries and any other supplies down the boardwalks. There're no cars there, you know?" She looked at me with a bit of crazy in her eye. Crazy then turned to sympathetic.

"Oh, Jane, I feel so sorry for you about Robert," this know-it-all said.

"Feel sorry for me about my son?" I barked back.

"Fire Island is a place where *homosexuals* go to meet other people." I hated the way she said the word. She acted as if I had just walked out of the cornfields. I could have killed Robert for not telling me, not because I was mad about where he was going but because this moron with a bad perm was trying to belittle me—at the Jewel-Osco, no less. But once again, I learned something about the gay lifestyle.

After telling her that she could stick her cantaloupe in a very uncomfortable place, I decided to do a little research on Fire Island.

I went home and got on the computer, something I wasn't all that comfortable with, but Robert had been teaching me over the phone. I typed "Fire Island" into the search thingy and I clicked on a few sites that were for adults only. Pretty dirty stuff, if you ask me. Finally, I reached one that sounded a little better.

There was an article by someone called Martha Stewslut, a faux Martha Stewart in the form of a drag queen. I wasn't thrilled that someone was messing with the domestic queen that is Martha. I liked her. Tough cookie, but I still liked her. Anyway, as I read on, this woman gave step-by-step instructions on how to make a chocolate torte, which irritated me because I was on Weight Watchers and this would surely put me over the limit. I clicked on some images of the island, and it was beautiful.

I looked at the Web site further and was puzzled. Robert hates to cook. Was $3500 worth it for a nice but not spectacular beach view? Not for Robert. This wasn't his scene. Although I had an idea from my run-in at the grocery store why he wanted to venture to this magic island.

Two weeks after his first visit to the house, I had my answer. Robert called to say he had met a man named Angelo. He even e-mailed me a picture. That was a big step for both of us, as I never knew how to download a picture before.

But seriously, it was finally a face. This was the first guy Robert had ever told me about, and it wasn't just some phantom. It was an Italian face, with stubble. He was very cute. Kind of reminded me of a cross between Sylvester Stallone and a mobster. It made me wonder, are the dating rituals the same when it's two men as they are with one man and one woman? I would think so. Robert said "sort of," except for the first date, when you do the dance of finding out who's a "top" and who's a "bottom." I didn't want to know any more in that arena.

I knew Robert would be a great catch for someone. He was

raised in a good home and had good morals, Catholic schools and everything.

Robert would tell me about the dates he would have with Angelo. Dinner on the beach, long walks by the ocean, dancing, and the parties they'd go to together. He was having more fun than I was! I've been married for thirty-seven years, but don't mistake me for some old lady. I got married at seventeen, and I am *only* fifty-three. Yes, I said *only*. Anyway, I love the details he gives me (well, to a degree). My husband was the only man I really dated, so I don't know what it's like to date. I think that is another reason Robert shares things with me. He lets me live each experience with him, as opposed to some children, who barely communicate with their parents. Not to sound too much like a self-help lady, but communication really is the key to any successful relationship, whether it's with your spouse or your child. Granted, he didn't tell me everything, just a few things.

Apparently, Angelo knew a thing or two about communication, and Robert got his first taste of rejection. He was devastated. I'd been through the tears of crying over boyfriends with my daughter, but I never thought I'd be dealing with it with my son. That was a weird experience. It felt good (but weird) when I told him, "Men are jerks." I felt like I was breaking some secret code of the women's society or something. As I listened to my heartbroken son, all I could think about was how I could get somebody to break this guy's legs. How could he be so mean? What a jerk.

CHAPTER NINE

Blue Day

A feeling you should never, ever, tell your mother about—unless you want a daily barrage of mail, e-mail, and phone calls checking on your mental well-being

After navigating myself out of Fire Island and my summer "relationship"—I use that term loosely, since two weekends a month for three months can hardly be considered a relationship—I was feeling even lower than before my first gay summer camp experience. My mother sensed it and began calling twice a day, each call more intense than the last.

"Are you sure you are okay?" she asked.

"I'm fine," I said while shoveling a box of Mrs. Fields double chocolate chip cookies into my mouth. To hell with Weight Watchers and the friggin' points. Who needs them?

After a few days (well, perhaps weeks), I thought I was fine. Then, one day, *it* arrived in the mail. It was a small, very official-looking manila envelope, but with soft handwriting that I instantly recognized. I pulled back the tab and gently opened it. With my mother I never knew what to expect. It could've been anything—a cheerful card, a photo of me and my dog Barney. I was expecting something jolly. What I opened was more shocking than anything else that I'd opened before. It was small in size, six-by-six inches, to be exact. And it was blue . . . with a giant frog staring directly at me. Large blue block letters read, *The Blue Day Book: A Lesson in Cheering Yourself Up.* What in God's name had she sent me?

Included inside were various pictures of animals in "wacky" poses, positioned so unnaturally that I seriously thought about calling PETA. Under each photo was a caption meant to be inspirational.

However, they only made me more irritable and depressed. I went back to the inside jacket of the book—$9.95 ($14.95 in Canada). As a struggling writer, this just about sent me over the edge. Here I was working as a mere publicist during the days while coming home in the evenings devoting hours to developing my craft of writing, and I get a book by some lovey-dovey sap that sells for friggin' nine dollars and ninety-five cents! On the cover it proudly proclaimed, "*New York Times* best-selling author." Were they playing some sort of sick and twisted joke on me? I'm sure this guy was making a fortune (a fortune and a half if he lived in Canada). People like my mother actually spent money on a book filled with animals looking sad and depressed, with lines like "There are miserable days when you feel lousy, grumpy . . ." Call me pessimistic, but I don't need to compare my life struggles to those of the hippo! A penguin, maybe, but not a hippo.

When I was upset as a kid, my mother would offer to take me to McDonald's to wash my blues down with a vanilla milkshake, two plain cheeseburgers, and a large order of french fries. Whether it actually took my depression away, I'm not sure, but usually I'd go into some sort of food coma and wouldn't be able to think of anything at all. It drove my mother nuts that we had to wait for specially made plain cheeseburgers. "Why can't you just scrape off the pickles, onions, ketchup, and mustard?" she'd ask.

"It's not the same. My burger tastes nasty after it touches those things," I'd argue. She'd curse the whole time the cashier would tell us to pull to the yellow line. I was happy that I wasn't the only one who had such refined culinary tastes. They had designated a whole section for us, the yellow line. "It's a goddamn joke that we have to wait twenty minutes," my mother would say. On the days my mother didn't feel like waiting, she'd send my father, who happily went along each time, forgetting what the previous experience had been like. He would eventually realize this was all strangely familiar after we'd been sitting in our car at the yellow line for twenty-three minutes. "I don't remember it taking this long the last time," he'd say.

"No, it must be a new person training," I'd say, knowing that the last time it actually took twenty-eight minutes.

"Right," he'd agree.

My parents were the type to do anything to cheer me up. Once, when I was in grade school, Chad Thomas had a huge party for the class and invited everyone but me and a few others. "I just don't have the room," he said. I was devastated. When I told my parents, they were enraged, and their rage quickly turned into action. Within two weeks, I had my own party in which my entire class but Chad Thomas was invited. It was no ordinary party. My mother went to Mike's Market and got the best cookies for the party, the fancy ones, not the iced animal crackers that they'd supposedly had at Chad's party. We had games and *real* prizes, not those stupid papier-mâché party favors that his mother had. At my bash, we gave out Hulk Hogan and the stars of the WWF wrestling dolls. The party was a huge success, and everyone talked about it for the next week at school. I had finally achieved popularity and fame in the sixth grade. Unfortunately, after that, Chad launched a full-on attack and had a slumber party complete with a guest appearance by Mark Ketchum, the high school's star basketball player and the best friend of Chad's older brother. I couldn't compete, so I threw in the towel. F. U., Chad.

I was much older now and on Weight Watchers, so McDonald's was no longer an option, nor was throwing a big party. I couldn't imagine my parents hosting a party with a bunch of gay men in their living room competing for a doll—unless, of course, the WWF dolls were replaced by the Dress and Play Britney Spears doll or Billy, the world's first anatomically correct gay doll, both of which I found equally revolting. However, I'm sure if I'd asked, my parents would have done it just to cheer me up.

There I sat in my Manhattan apartment with a depressed frog staring me in the face. I couldn't believe my mother, my own flesh and blood, would subject me to such infantile material. Did she honestly think a bunch of depressed animals were going to make me feel better? I opened the book and began reading the text from the beginning. There was nothing there that was life changing or even new to me. As I leafed through the book, the animals became more optimistic with every page. Then, out of nowhere, these "happy, well-adjusted" animals became ecstatic, because they were now with a *mate*, somebody to love them. All this did was remind me why I was depressed in the first place. Now even the goddamn animals had somebody. This sent me over the edge. I threw the book on the floor and swore I'd never get a pet. I took a walk around my neighborhood cursing every animal that crossed my path.

I wandered for what seemed like hours. I thought I was out of my mini-depression, but thanks to my mother's reminder that I was alone, I was right back in it. I wandered through the crowded streets of New York and eventually spotted the Golden Arches in the middle of Times Square. Sanctuary. I knew I was on a "program," and I knew I was trying to get in better shape, but all of that went out the window. I walked inside and instantly recognized the smell of potatoes in a deep fryer. I was home again.

I waited in line with a nervous excitement, as if I was doing something devilishly bad. I glanced at the menu to see if there had been any changes since we'd last met. Although there were a few additions, the basics were still there. I was so proud of my arches for "keeping it real." I was next, and I gave the unhappy lady my order. "Yes, hi!" I gushed. "It's been a long time." The cashier looked at me as if I were one of the crazies off the street. (She was only half right.) "Anyway, I'd like a large vanilla shake, a large order of french fries, and two *plain* cheeseburgers," I said, near the point of orgasm.

"That'll be $9.86," she said. Prices had indeed gone up since my last visit. "Step to the yellow counter." To my sheer amazement, even in New York you were instructed to step aside to wait for your special order. I smiled, remembering the days with my dad. Ahhh, yes, I was finally feeling better, and I hadn't even taken a McBite.

My smile soon turned to a plastic grin as the minutes went by. The plastic grin was replaced by a stony countenance, followed by rocking back and forth on the balls of my feet. Twenty-six minutes later, my meal finally was brought out to me. Actually, it was thrown at me in a bag.

I practically skipped back to my apartment with my treasure in hand. (Yes, I said skip.) I got inside and immediately plopped down on the couch. Then, I put my entire meal on a plate and just stared at it, taking in every smell. My worries melted away like the grease melting into the paper that covered my burger. I picked up *The Blue Day Book* again and started reading. This time it was different. The animals were cute, and the text below was witty. I loved the polar bear pretending to do yoga. The zebra laughing was genius. The mouse on the cat's head was suddenly poignant. This man was a literary genius—he had captured my range of emotions in ninety-two pages and less than one hundred sentences.

Nearly thirty minutes passed, and I found myself lying on the couch smirking, remembering all the silly moments at home with my parents. I looked down at my plate and to my surprise, I hadn't eaten a thing! It wasn't the food that I needed; it was the comfort of home and the reminder that all I needed to do when I got into a tailspin was to take myself out of my own head. I soon realized that the twenty or so odd minutes that McDonald's makes you wait is actually the perfect amount of time to recollect your thoughts and put life back into perspective. It was a McTherapy session—and cheap, too, relatively speaking.

In that space of time, I realized that my summer romance with

Angelo was much like the cheeseburgers I'd always ordered as a kid. In this case, though, I had made the mistake of not specifying a *plain* cheeseburger without all the extras covering everything up. Next time, I'll wait the additional twenty minutes to get what I actually want.

Mama Says

After his rejection, I thought a lot about how I could make Robert believe there are a lot of guys in the sea. I stopped in the bookstore and walked through the aisles, not really sure what I was doing there. Then a little blue book called out to me. It was small in size, but I knew it packed a powerful punch. I leafed through it and it seemed perfect. It was something I knew he'd get instantly—a book about how even whales, dogs, and cats always end up with someone in the end. I wanted to show him that even a whale could find a mate. I thought it would do the trick. Several angry phone calls later, I realized that maybe this wasn't the best choice of books to cheer him up.

No couple has a perfect relationship—I don't care if you're straight or gay. We all have to give and take and find out who the other person is and what he or she is about. Dr. Phil might call it something else; I just call it what it is, plain and simple: *Let's Make a Deal*. The basic premise of that show was that the contestant made a choice between prizes behind three doors. Some were really fantastic and some were not so great. The person could either take the sure thing or gamble that they would get something better. Life is no different. At several pivotal moments in a person's life, choices present themselves. One can risk everything and either reap the rewards or lose it all based solely on the promise of better things to come.

I've learned that at some stages in life, it's better to take what you've got and walk away, and in others it's better to take a chance and open yourself up to something new. (I have been stuck in a couple of stages in my lifetime.) My husband worked hard to support a family; my job was to take care of the kids and get them through the stages of their lives. Our family comes first, in case you haven't noticed.

Perhaps the lesson realized for Robert was not to be distracted by the physical and ignore the character. I *hope* he learned not to look for a boyfriend on an island of gay men—even I know that, and I've never been there.

I sound like I have all the answers, but I don't. One thing's for sure—I do know my son. These were all the things I was trying to say to him then but couldn't put into words. So I did what any mother would do: I sent him a picture book filled with whales, dogs, and cats who find love. Yes, reading that sentence back makes me sound like a lunatic, but come on, who doesn't love puppies? If that doesn't make you smile, your heart is made of stone.

CHAPTER TEN
It's Getting Hot in Here

Famous lyric in a song by rapper Nelly, or what my mother says after having too many cosmopolitans (one, to be exact)

Like the rest of the flock, my mom and I were on our way to New York's latest trendy restaurant, Cafeteria, to meet my friend Freddy (a.k.a. "The Mayor," so named because there wasn't a person he didn't know). I wanted to give my mom a true New York experience. Cafeteria is sleek and trendy. The wait staff's clothes were designer. An avant-garde architect had designed the space-age, gleaming white restaurant. Madonna had been there. Enough said.

My mother was excited to be going but balked at the restaurant's name and concept. "I just think it's dumb. How many people do you know who've had good memories of anything with the name Cafeteria?" she complained during the cab ride. As much as I hated to admit it because Cafeteria was the current destination of all things cool, she was right. Only in New York would you wait weeks in advance to get a table, sit in an obscenely loud room, and pay triple the price for food you cringed at when the lunch lady dumped it on your plate. Yet, I was willing to throw my cafeteria flashbacks all out the window to show her a good time. (In all honesty, I had ulterior motives. Cafeteria was in Chelsea, and it seemed to be *the* dinner place for every hot, available gay man. Yes, I was about to cruise with my mother. Sad but true.)

My mother and I were right on time, a major faux pas in New York circles and an even bigger faux pas in the gay fashionista hangouts like this one. The hostess gave us that "Oh, so glad to see you" roll of the eyes and guided us through the loud, bustling restaurant and down the stairs into a quaint, dimly lit room with eight tables cramped next to one another.

The "bitch who needed to eat," as my mother called her, sat us at a small table in the corner, adjacent to a large banquette of well-to-do gay men. I rushed to sit down and ogle the banquette. I explained to my mother that I often played "Name that Loon," a game I created while sitting alone at coffee shops during my first few months living in the Big Apple. The rules are quite simple and the game can be played anywhere. The goal is to figure out each person's story at the table, including who earned the title of "a few sandwiches short of a picnic," or, in more civilized circles, "certifiable nut job." Trust me, every table has one.

While my mother fussed in her seat, I scanned the table. I speculated that the conservative-looking guy probably liked to be tied up and whipped, while the guy with the sleeveless shirt was sleeping with the conservative-looking guy's boyfriend. Yet none of them earned the sash of "the loon," meaning the handsome man with the button-down earned the title by default. He had one of those crazy laughs—I'm not talking about somebody who laughs louder than everybody else, but a person who laughs longer than everybody while his eyes have that sinister "I eat scabs when I'm home alone" look. Figuring out this table took all of three minutes, but I suddenly feared that both my mother and I were being sized up as the restaurant's biggest loons by *their* table.

What I failed to mention was that instead of chairs at our mini-tables, my mother and I were sitting awkwardly on Styrofoam eggs.

"Is there a problem?" the waitress asked.

"We look beyond ridiculous," my mother said to our waitress as she grasped the edge of the table to keep her balance. Our waitress tried to explain to my Midwestern mother that this was apparently the latest craze in furniture design. "A horizontal egg? Who designs these things? Probably some idiot who never has to sit on them. I feel like I'm about to give birth here," my mother said with a shrug. The skinny wannabe model-cum-waitress stared blankly at her, a look I was confident she'd spent hours practicing in front of the mirror so when she finally got on the runway she could be devoid of any emotion whatsoever. I could pull off the same face if I wanted to; it was no big deal. I'd perfected that look while experiencing the joys of Vicodin after having foot surgery, but no one had knocked on my door to model.

"Can we have two cosmos—immediately?" I shouted before my mother was able to go on a full assault.

My mother looked around at the small room in the lower level of this *trés chic* restaurant, looked me dead in the eyes, and said, "I don't get it. It feels like we're in a basement. What's the big deal?" Even though I knew that fundamentally I agreed with what she was saying (as I'd often thought the same thing, but never said it out loud), I still had to go along with the lie that this place deserved to be the coolest restaurant in New York City.

I lifted the small bowl. "Have a chip and relax," I said. She reached into the bowl and inspected what appeared to be fried air. "This looks like pork rinds," she said matter-of-factly. She took a bite. "Spicy!" she said while chewing before going into a serious coughing fit. The table of "loons" stared us down.

We needed something fast or I knew I'd lose her to boredom or, worse yet, sleep. Luckily, the cocktail waitress appeared with a round of cosmos courtesy of Freddy, who had phoned the restaurant to say he was running on "island" time. I knew Manhattan was an island, but this was definitely a stretch. My mother hesitated when the waitress set the drinks down.

"I don't know about this. You know I'm not a big drinker," she protested.

"Ma, just try it. You'll like it. Trust me. Besides, this is what they're always drinking on *Sex and the City*. You are a *Sex and the*

City girl," I teased. My mother, stylish as she may be, is definitely *not* a *Sex and the City* girl. But I could be wrong; maybe during her Weight Watchers meetings the four or five gathered women talk about their sex lives (but over chocolate éclairs instead of cosmos).

Three cosmos (and for my mother, three sheets to the wind) later, Freddy finally arrived with a small group of sophisticated and good-looking men. They were seated at a large banquette while we remained on the eggs.

"Wow, he's handsome," my mother blurted out loudly.

"He's gay," I whispered in her ear.

"So, I can't say he's handsome just because he's gay?" she asked in what she believed to be a whisper, but what in reality was more of a shriek.

Freddy made the introductions: Marc, a New York advertising titan; Ross, a very accomplished artist; and Rupert, as in *My Best Friend's Wedding*, Everett. *My Best Friend's Wedding* had come out roughly nine months prior, and his celebrity was rising, especially with the gay boys at Cafeteria. Rupert was the first gay character in a film that I actually liked. He was masculine, handsome, and smart, all the things I was looking for in a mate. I had an instant crush on him after seeing his gorgeous smile. Needless to say, I didn't even get a second look. Before I could feel sorry for myself, my mother, in almost a full shout, said, "Why do I know that guy?" I sank even deeper into my Styrofoam seat.

I looked at my mother, and I noticed that her face was growing flushed and she was beginning to sweat. I'd seen this face only three times before. The first was at my brother's wedding reception. The second, my sister's baby shower. The third was when I told my parents I wanted to move to New York, and on that occasion her face had been crimson. "It's hot in here," she repeated several times in a borderline slur. "It's hot in here" was code to my brother and sister that mom was buzzed/borderline drunk, and that in itself was a sight to behold. I excused myself to go to the restroom, partly to give her a minute to collect herself and partly for me to escape any potentially embarrassing outbursts in front of Rupert, not that he would have noticed me anyway.

I wasn't gone more than five minutes before I returned to find my mother sitting at the table with all of the "A-list" gays Freddy had brought. She was a hit. These boys loved her.

"I think you should dump that jerk," I heard her say to Marc.

"I love this one," Marc said to Freddy. "She has to come to our cocktail party next weekend, Lou."

My mother was not only buzzed, but she'd transformed herself into a bona fide hit right before my eyes. She sipped yet another cosmo as I sat back down on my egg.

I heard the waitress explaining the egg seats to another table. "It's an authentic Paulista," she said, whatever that meant. Her comment did, however, make me think about my own authenticity. As a kid trying to fit in, I was never sure just what group I fit into. I was basically friends with everybody yet friends with no one. I knew inside that I was gay, but there was no way I could tell anyone at a very small Catholic high school. I wanted to find people like me, but at the same time I was paranoid that I'd be branded gay, so I was always somewhere in the middle. Even though she didn't know what I was going through at the time, my mother gave me a valuable piece of advice that I still try to live my life by today: "The best way to meet people is to simply be authentic," she said. I didn't realize the truth of this advice until years later, while sipping cosmos in the basement of an ultra-trendy Manhattan restaurant. She wasn't impressed by the restaurant, the food, the waitstaff, or the semi-celebrities. She was just there being herself and enjoying a night out with her son.

I took a look around the room, which had filled to capacity with beautiful gay men sizing one another up, each one trying to be what he *thought* he should be. I took a deep breath and introduced myself to the other men at the table and bravely began to engage them in conversation. I gave up on playing it cool—even the coolest guy couldn't possibly look suave hatching a giant egg with my cosmo-infused mom—and I loved every single minute of it. Maybe she was more *Sex and the City* than I ever really knew.

Mama Says

Cosmopolitans. Two parts lemon-infused vodka. One part Coin-treau. Two parts cranberry. One old lady on the floor.

The concept of meeting people for drinks is completely foreign to me. Where I'm from, it's not often that you'd hear someone say, "Let's go meet for drinks." If that rare occasion were to occur, the choices of venue would be slim. There is the town's one and only restaurant, where the only people sitting having drinks are the ones who have been there since ten in the morning. That's pretty much it, unless you prefer to stand in the gas station parking lot and sip a beer. So when Robert said we were going to meet some friends of his for drinks, I wasn't sure what to expect.

I've never been a drinker. I got married at such an early age that I missed out on the whole social aspect of it. I tried drinking for the first time with my then boyfriend (and now husband) when I was fifteen. I hated it. I gave it a second chance when I went to Las Vegas at twenty with my mother for a getaway. I was turned away at the entrance to Caesar's Palace. I was too young to enter and I was too young to drink. Even my mother's complaints to the management didn't make them budge. They didn't care, so instead we had a very serene trip, as opposed to the blowout of fun we'd hoped for. It didn't matter that I was married and had two children at the time. These people clearly didn't understand that a mother needed a few drinks every now and then to avoid going certifiably insane. This time I was with my son, and he was going to show me a good time.

From what I remember—it's still foggy to this day—we went down to the basement of some restaurant that was supposed to be *the* hot place of the moment. Robert has always found a way to get into these places. It baffles me how he does it, because when he first moved to New York, he didn't know a soul, and roughly a year later he was taking his mother to a place I'd read about in *In Style* magazine on the plane. He had made jokes before about a "gay mafia," and sometimes I wondered if he was one of their capos. He was far too young to be a don, from what I'd seen in the movies.

We walked through the restaurant and went down the stairs by the kitchen. I didn't think they meant "hot spot" so literally. The hostess, or the "woman who thought she was on the runway," brought us into this room that looked like a fancy version of an igloo: white walls with ice-blue trim, white leather, and very low white lacquer tables. Robert called this place a "bar," but it was more like a basement to me, small and damp. Since the room was filling up, or because we didn't look quite cool enough, the wait-ress walked us right past the white leather booths. She handed Robert the menu and told him to enjoy. He smiled politely and pulled up an egg-shaped footstool and sat down while trying to look as comfortable as possible in a room full of stares. I think I'm a pretty hip lady, but the idea of sitting on a giant egg was not something I was prepared to do. Robert told me it was a part of the "New York experience." "If you're looking for warmth—in decor, staff, or customers—we can go to T.G.I. Friday's," he teased. So I maneuvered my way down on the egg, nearly falling three times. What I don't do for Berto.

I initially thought Robert and his friend Freddy were a couple; he talked so much about "The Mayor" that I just assumed that this was a new love interest for him. When Freddy finally arrived, my mouth about hit the floor, because what Robert neglected to mention was that Freddy is my age. I don't care how nice a man he might be; I don't want someone my age with my son. I took a deep breath and continued on with pleasant conversation, and this was after only one cosmo.

I was much chattier than usual, I noticed, but I didn't think a thing of it. Robert ordered another round, and again I hesitated. I don't drink much, maybe an occasional glass of wine; I just never found a drink I really liked. Well, after the third cosmo, I think I found that drink. I had to tell Freddy that Robert was much too young for him while my focus was still clear, but I was really enjoying myself, and it'd have to wait until later. After a while, even though I wasn't going through menopause, I thought I was having hot flashes, because it suddenly became very hot in there. Within a few minutes, I couldn't hear much of anything, just white noise. Robert smiled and said it was because of all the cosmos. Hell, at that point, I thought I was a part of the "cosmos."

Freddy introduced me to a lot of famous people that night, but please don't ask me who they were; I just can't remember. Rupert Everett kept smiling my way, or at least I thought he was. It turned out he was looking over me at the bartender. In fact, a lot of good-looking men were looking our way, and soon I realized their looks weren't meant for me. How was I supposed to know that he was gay in real life?

I'd never been in a situation like this. I didn't know where to look or what to do, so I continued to smile and sip another cosmo. Robert later told me most of the people in the bar that night were gay, which wasn't a news flash after the first thirty minutes. I might have been tipsy, but I had figured that out. I told Robert I couldn't tell who was gay and who wasn't—that if I were young and single, I'd be flirting.

My moment finally came when Robert excused himself to go to the toilet. I clumsily got off my egg and sat my ass down next to

Freddy to find out what exactly was going on between him and my son.

"Look," I said, "you are a really fun man, and hell, if I were a gay guy, I'd go for you." Freddy smiled and looked at me as if he knew where this was going. "If you really like my son, that's one thing, but if you are just using him for arm candy, I won't have it. I've seen too many men do that to women that I know, and I'm not going to let a man do it to my own son," I explained calmly. Freddy stared and smiled like the Cheshire cat. He let me know that I couldn't have been more wrong and that the two of them were definitely not an item. They were good friends, and Robert looked to him as a guide through this "crazy gay existence." I took another huge sigh of relief and chased it with a gulp of cosmo.

"Wow, you're tough, lady! Can you inspect my boyfriend and tell me if he's on the up and up?" Marc, the advertising bigwig, shouted across the table. Everyone laughed, and we made a toast. Robert came back downstairs and wasn't sure what to make of it all. He sat quietly and just smiled at me while I sat with a group of men that were all my age but definitely not interested in anything I had to offer. This was yet again another experience I had never imagined sharing with my son, but I wouldn't have changed it for the world.

I needed to get some air, so I asked Robert if we could leave the "lunchroom" behind and walk home instead of taking a cab, as I was afraid I'd be sick. We walked down Seventh Avenue with the lights from Times Square gleaming behind us. Yes, it was no doubt a "New York experience," as Robert liked to call it, but I'd like to think of it more as a Robert/Jane, mother/son experience, at one with the cosmos, or was it cosmos?

CHAPTER ELEVEN

Are You In or Are You Out?

Long before *Project Runway* and Heidi Klum, there was my mother

Ms. D was a rising star that I met through another publicist friend. We'll call her Ms. D, for diva of course. I'm not sure why, but Ms. D immediately took to me and I found her wildly entertaining. I think I was the only one that tolerated her horrifyingly honest nature. I know on more than one occasion she made her publicist cry.

He was forty-two.

Ms. D called me one night after I was ready to curl up on my couch after a long day at work and a rigorous workout at my gym. She'd just broken up with her boyfriend, someone she thought was "the one."

"How are you doing?" I asked in my most sympathetic tone. We didn't really have the kind of relationship where we cried on one another's shoulders, but I thought perhaps she was reaching out to take our friendship to a new level.

"Fine, I suppose."

"Is there anything I can do? Do you need anything? We can rent a funny movie. I could just sit with you if you want me to do that. I can also get some soup for you."

There was a long pause. I assumed that Ms. D was sobbing and trying to compose herself.

"Are you there, honey?" I asked. "Let it out. You'll feel better."

"I was taking a puff from my cigarette," she said, and exhaled.

"Oh."

"A. I don't want to rent a funny movie with you. That sounds just plain awful. B. You want to 'sit' with me? I'll pass. C. And soup? You've got to be kidding me. I was dumped. I don't have mono."

I didn't nickname her Ms. D because of her cheery disposition.

"I thought you needed comforting. Those were the only things I could think of," I said.

"This is not *Beaches* nor am I a fat girl. I don't need you to have a vagina, Robert. I need you to have a penis, for once."

"I'm pretty sure I got that covered. You obviously called me for some reason other than to berate me? Or was that part of the plan to make yourself feel better?"

"No, that's an added bonus that I'm especially enjoying. What are you doing tonight?" she asked. Before I could answer, she jumped in. "Who am I kidding? You're staying in. Come to a movie premiere with me," she said.

"I hate you," I said.

"Now is that how you talk to your friend who was unceremoniously dumped only hours before?" Ms. D barked.

"No, I suppose not."

I realize that going out with Ms. D probably sounds like torture to most, but in some strange way the masochist in me found her incredibly amusing. She had more pithy, nasty remarks than any bitter gay man I knew. She whined and complained incessantly everywhere we went. There was never a time when I saw her reach for the check when we were out. As I listened to Ms. D talk in detail about what she expected out of this night, it dawned on me why her boyfriend broke up with her: she was an asshole.

But she was mine, for better or worse. The thing about Ms. D is that she actually can be quite fun. She's gorgeous, which means beautiful straight men attempt to flirt with her and gay boys try to audition for the role of her new gay best friend. Either way, I knew I'd be surrounded by a lot of available guys. The other thing about her was that she's absolutely hilarious, and will say whatever she's thinking whenever she feels like it. Some referred to her as "the devil" or a "bitch," and I simply called her "my friend."

"And don't try and tell me that you can't make it, you were ready to weep and wail with me on the couch no more than thirty seconds ago," she said.

"I guess I could come."

"Really with the 'I guess'? Come on, spare me the internal debate of staying at home on your couch and watching *Seinfeld* reruns or going to a premiere." Truth be told I was leaning heavily towards *Seinfeld*.

"I'm only going for you," I said.

"Yeah, yeah, yeah. Anyway, I'll pick you up on the way. They're sending me a town car. Oh, and dress butch," she added.

"Um, because I normally would wear a dress? Why would you even say that to me?"

Silence.

"Hello?"

An hour later, Ms. D picked me up. I kissed her hello and gave her a giant hug in the backseat.

"I'm so sorry about today. Look at it this way: You're now going to be open to meet the right guy. Everything happens for a reason and you may not know what that reason is yet, but you'll figure it out. Any man would be lucky to call you his girlfriend," I said, and squeezed her hand.

Our eyes met and I was sure that she was nearly moved to tears by my support. She opened her mouth and said, "Listen, I'm going to need you to really be extra masculine when we walk the press line. I don't want everyone thinking I took my gay friend to this premiere."

I don't know why I bothered.

"Ms. D, what does that mean exactly? This is the second time you've made reference to my masculinity and, furthermore, why would it be a bad thing that you took your gay friend to a movie premiere? Frankly, your image could use some softening."

"Oh, don't get your panties in a bunch. I'm not directing this at you personally. However, I don't want to be known as the sad little fag-hag who got dumped. No thank you."

"That is the dumbest thing I've heard you say, and you've said some really stupid things in the short time that I've known you."

"I was just dumped by the love of my life," she said as her face turned from condescending and mean to being on the verge of tears.

It's hard watching someone you care about, or anyone for that matter, go through the emotions of a breakup. It made me think about my own life and how I would feel if the person I thought I'd be with for the rest of my life suddenly said, "I'm not attracted to you anymore. I don't find you sexy." Oh, I didn't mention that part? Yeah, that's what he said to her. It was because of this that I went along with whatever Ms. D wanted.

"Fine," I said before letting out a giant sigh. "Do you want me to grab my crotch on the red carpet to really spice it up?" I laughed.

"Okay, straight guys don't say crotch or use phrases like 'spice it up.' Maybe you shouldn't speak."

"Oh come on, I passed as straight for twenty-one years, I'm pretty sure I can do it for a couple of hours," I said. Ms. D arched her very plucked eyebrow. "What? I will give you names and phone numbers of people that believed I was straight."

"Save it, Ellen DeGeneres," she said and looked out the window. "It looks like we're almost there." She lowered her head again and started texting.

The car slowed down and the closer we got to the theater the more nervous I became. *Maybe I couldn't pull off this charade again after all?* Ms. D was too busy texting to notice the beads of sweat forming on my forehead.

The car came to a stop. "Here we go," Ms. D said, and smiled at me. I smiled back at her, glad that I did the unselfish thing and decided to be there for her despite her bad behavior. She leaned over and kissed me and put her hand on my knee. In a sweet and soft almost Betty White–like voice, she said to me, "Don't fuck it up."

The driver came around to open the door for Ms. D. She stepped out gracefully, looking every bit the star that she is. She was born to do exactly this. I climbed across the backseat and was nearly out of the car when I lost my balance and came hurtling out. I felt like Uncle Fester from *The Addams Family*.

Ms. D grabbed my arm and we strolled up Broadway and waited to hit the red carpet. As we stopped for the celebrity on the carpet to move through the press line, I couldn't help but think that I didn't have a chance in hell of pulling this act off. I was embarrassed that I was even pretending to be something that I wasn't. It had taken so much emotional strength to finally admit who I was. I felt like a sham. I realized that acting wasn't my thing. It was for the people on the carpet.

"Okay, we ready?" Ms. D asked. I nodded and she wrapped her arm around mine and we took a step. Ms. D turned and looked at me and stopped. She squeezed my arm and smiled. "I got this."

"Really?" I asked.

"I'll see you on the other side," she said and turned her back to me. The flashbulbs went crazy and I took my place out of their glare. Bullet dodged.

Then I saw *him*.

While I stood off to the side and let Ms. D be photographed by the legions of paparazzi, an incredibly attractive guy was at the other end of the red carpet. We locked eyes and I felt a surge of adrenaline course through my body. He was stunning. I had to meet him. Call it confidence or the need to make out with a hot guy, but to Ms. D's surprise I grabbed her arm and quickly walked the press line to where my future husband was waiting.

"What the hell was that?" she said as we walked into the lobby.

Before I could answer, a young woman wearing a headset approached Ms. D. "Give us a second," Ms. D said.

"No problem, I have your tickets when you're ready to go inside," the young brunette said and went to speak to another headset-clad woman.

"You told me to butch it up, so I grabbed my woman to go inside," I said in a whisper.

"Hey, buddy, I'm here for the press, not for the shitty movie," she said.

I was about to speak when I saw him again, the guy on the red carpet. Now he was standing exactly in the same spot where I was only a few minutes before. *Was he looking for me?*

Ms. D continued to drone on. "How else is *he* supposed to know that this breakup meant nothing to me if there's no pictures of me out?" Then my future lover stepped to the side and I let out an audible gasp.

"Well, that was masculine," Ms. D said under her breath.

"Well, Sally Sunshine," I said, "apparently the two of you had the same idea because he just stepped onto the red carpet with a hot blonde." My paramour was walking Ms. D's ex and his date up the red carpet.

"Oh my God. I gotta go!" she said and darted up the escalator after the young woman who had our tickets.

"Publicity girl!" she shouted as she darted up the moving steps. "Hello! Publicity girl!"

I hung out in the lobby by myself for the next fifteen minutes or so people watching, and *maybe* I was also waiting for the hot guy to walk by me again. I was relieved to be away from Ms. D, even if it was only momentarily. With still no sign of my mystery man and as the crowd began to swell, I left to go find my seat. If there was one thing I couldn't stand more than Ms. D's verbal assault, it was large crowds. I walked toward the escalators and reached into my pocket for my ticket.

Nada.

Three girls dressed in black suits and holding clipboards looked at me as though I was a suicide bomber.

"Sir, can I help you?" the taller one said.

"I don't seem to have my ticket," I said casually. The young woman looked me in the face and spoke into her headset.

"Becky, can you come over here, please. There's a gentleman here who doesn't seem to have his ticket," she said. This was followed by a rapid-fire stream of "uh-huhs," "yeps," and "got its" without ever taking her eyes off of me.

Then the woman on her left suddenly started speaking to me while the lead girl continued to stare at me. "Sir, if you could just step over here, someone will be with you in a moment." I thought I was going to be taken in the back room and beaten.

Finally, another woman appeared out of nowhere and introduced herself as Becky. She was very high-strung and sweaty as she looked me up and down. She raised her eyebrows without saying hello. It was the kind of look that says, "Who's the loser party-crasher?"

After a few awkward moments of me waiting for her to say something, I finally spoke. "Hi, my date had an emergency and ran off with my ticket." I tried giving her my best Midwestern charm and moved in closer. "Is there any way you could let me in?"

She had a look of terror on her face, a look that I was all too familiar with when I worked at other PR firms. Being so close to Becky, I finally noticed that her dress was ill-fitting, her hair was slightly off, and I knew she probably hadn't had eight hours of sleep in at least a year. This was normal for a publicity assistant. I saw myself in her. I thought about what it must be like for this young studio publicist to go through life feeling on edge from morning till night. I thought maybe I could pull her aside and talk to her about work, give her advice and pointers on what I learned while working at several other PR jobs, if for no other reason than to escape the fate of becoming an angry, bitter person. I wished someone had done that for me. I smiled at her warmly, ready to dispense my wisdom, when suddenly she spoke.

"Are you fucking kidding me right now? Do you honestly expect me to believe that? No way. Absolutely not."

Too late.

"Wow. Okay, then. I was with Ms. D," I said politely.

"Ms. D? Uh-huh," she said.

"Yes, Ms. D," I said.

"And where is your friend Ms. D now?" she sniped.

I don't believe in violence of any sort, but I was about to start gouging myself in the ear so I wouldn't have to hear Becky's snotty tone any longer.

"Seriously, ask any of the press standing out on the carpet and they'll tell you," I explained.

"There are other guests waiting to get in. You're going to have to have your 'friend' come out and get you," Becky said. "Or you could just call her. Oh, but wait, I bet you don't have her number, do you?"

Becky wasn't like me at all. She actually enjoyed being mean. She had to be stopped.

"First of all, can you please not talk to me like that?" I said. She didn't say a word. "My friend isn't getting reception inside of the theater," I argued. "I've tried calling her three times, but thanks for that helpful suggestion, genius."

"Sir, you're going to have to move to let our guests with tickets inside," she said, holding her clipboard.

Becky probably had no idea when she moved to New York and got what she thought was a fabulous PR job that her life was going to be hell. She was probably a nice girl at one time, even laid-back—a person that I may have even wanted to befriend. I silently predicted that she would be addicted to prescription pills within three months. It gave me some relief.

Before I went completely crazy, I heard a man's voice from behind me.

"Actually, Becky, he was on the carpet with Ms. D," the voice said. I turned around and saw the tall man with beautiful dark hair and blue eyes. I think he might have looked inside my soul at that very moment. It was quite possible.

"Thank you!" I said, loud enough for whomever was close enough to hear Becky's tirade on me. I looked at this dashingly handsome man and nodded my head in agreement, which didn't actually make sense with the words coming out of my mouth. It didn't matter because I wanted Becky to know that he and I were in total sync, even though we had just met.

I looked back at Becky, who attempted to hide her anger at this latest development. "Thanks, Becky!" I said with a giant smile on my face.

"I'll walk you in," my new husband said.

"What's your name?" I asked.

"I'm Ryan," he said and extended his hand for me to shake. I shook his hand and he held it a little longer than most normal handshakes. There was an obvious and undeniable connection.

"I'm Robert," I said and looked him dead in the eye.

"So you're her escort tonight?" Ryan asked.

"Escort? I'm not a hooker," I said.

"No, I meant you escorted her here," he said. "Sorry, I didn't mean to . . ."

"It's okay. I mean, I'm flattered and all that you think I'm cute enough to be a hooker, but I'm not," I said.

Ryan wasn't sure what to make of me. "You're a good date nonetheless," he said.

"I am?" I asked. "Yes, I mean, I am."

"So Ms. D left you out here in the cold, huh? You must be in the doghouse," he said and laughed.

"Uh, yeah. I guess," I said and shrugged. "She actually saw one of her exes getting ready to walk the red carpet with you and . . ."

I stopped mid-sentence. I regretted saying this the minute it left my mouth. Apparently, I was such a sucker for nice eyes, a great smile, and a banging body that I sold out my quasi-friend for them.

"Anyway . . . do you see my date anywhere?" I asked, looking around the concession stand. People were picking up complimentary soda and popcorn on their way inside. There was still no sign of Ms. D. I looked at Ryan again. God, he was hot. I didn't care if I ever saw her again.

"I don't see her. Maybe she's in the bathroom. Would you like me to wait with you?" he said, holding his eyes on me for a moment longer than normal. I knew this game. He was interested. OH. MY. GOD. He was interested in *me*!

"That would be amazing," I said, a little too excited. I quickly corrected myself. "Yeah, I guess that would be cool. I'm sure she'll be out any minute."

"That's quite a girlfriend you have," Ryan said.

I knew that I was at a crossroads when Ryan called Ms. D my girlfriend. "Umm, well, she is quite a woman," I said, ignoring his moniker for Ms. D.

I weighed the pros and cons of telling the truth about Ms. D, but I knew that if I exposed her, I would have spent the next two hours apologizing to her for ruining her ruse all in the hopes that I would get a date. It wouldn't be the right thing to do and she did just suffer a breakup. She needed me to pretend I was her date and I was going to fulfill that request even if it killed me. I looked at Ryan as he spoke into his headset. *Damn you, Ms. D.*

"She's not my girlfriend," I blurted out as if I had just caught a case of Tourette's syndrome. Ms. D would have to get over it: There was a boy involved.

"Whoa." Ryan looked at me curiously. In a nervous panic, I had apparently shouted this fact.

"Also, I'm gay," I said, still shouting as he walked closer to me.

"Okay, and now the publicity department at the studio knows that, too," Ryan said, and shook his head.

I smiled nervously and found myself spitting out random nonsequential sentences left and right. "She didn't have a date and asked me to go. She needed to show up with someone because her ex was going to be here. She's just a friend!"

Now don't get me wrong, Ms. D had thrown me under the bus several other times for her own benefit. We were once in an elevator that gradually got more and more crowded, something Ms. D absolutely hated since she was slightly claustrophobic. Not only did she suffer from this affliction, but it also resulted in a nervous stomach. As Ms. D stared at the ground willing the entire elevator to go unnoticed, she also emitted the most foul-smelling gas that I've come across to this day. It was so bad that I considered getting off of the elevator and walking the twenty-six floors to the lobby. Sensing the gagging motions of the other passengers, Ms. D turned to me and said, "That is revolting. I will never understand men." Not only did she blame me for her odor, but she blamed my entire gender.

I asked her about it later in the car and she told me, "I don't fart. Got that? If ever there is a minor gas explosion near me, it came from you, not me. We clear?"

So as I stood in the Sony Lincoln Square movie theater I verbally farted with regard to Ms. D's personal life. However, Ryan didn't seem interested in Ms. D. He was, on the other hand, suddenly very interested in my sexuality.

"So you're openly gay?" Ryan asked.

"Yes, aren't you?" I asked and smiled.

"Yeah," Ryan said as his face dropped. His eyes darted all around the theater, avoiding mine.

"Awesome!" I said, wondering what was going on.

Ryan didn't immediately respond to what I said. When he finally did, he said in the most aloof way possible, "Yeah, I guess. So listen, I don't think this is going to work out." It was as if we broke up before we even got started.

"Wait, I'm sorry, what? What do you mean?" I asked.

By the way he reacted, you would have thought I told him that I had a raging case of herpes. He laid into me with an uncomfortable fake smile that made him look like he was in desperate need of a bathroom. I stood there and looked at him, confused.

"So obviously, you like masculine guys," I said.

He nodded his head.

"And obviously I must be masculine enough for you since you thought I was heterosexual. So, I'm not really sure what the problem is here," I said. Ryan had clearly been down this road before or had imagined it in some kind of porn. Either way, my gayness was a huge disappointment to this gay man.

"Yeah . . ." he said, trailing off. "I better get back to work. Enjoy the movie," he said and turned his back and walked down the long hallway.

Enjoy the movie? Was he kidding me? No "I'll see you at the after-party?"

That was it? I had to think quickly. I decided the best approach was to calmly see what I did wrong. I remained standing in the same place, not wanting to scare him by running up behind him to continue our talk. I knew Ryan would come around, but I didn't want to have to wait until the after-party for him to answer the clue phone.

"You only wanted me if you thought I was straight? I can go

back in the closet! I'll do it if that's what you want!" I shouted from the other end of the hallway. Subtle, I know. To my complete surprise, Ryan never turned around.

I went into the theater to find Ms. D and take my seat. Of course, when I spotted her my chair was taken by someone that she previously had a crush on. By this time the movie was about to begin and the director was speaking to the packed house. I grabbed an usher and together we found the last available seat—in the front row.

After the movie ended, I waited for Ms. D outside of the theater.

"Where were you?" Ms. D asked, suddenly concerned.

"You ran off with my ticket when you didn't want to see 'Kitty Meow,'" I said, turning my body toward her. Ms. D called her ex Kitty Meow when they dated so no one would discover their secret relationship. I didn't get the nickname, either, but after the first time I heard her say it to me, I decided that I hated cats.

"Why are you moving like an idiot? You look ridiculous," she said.

"Oh, am I? I had to sit in the front row of the movie theater thanks to you. I sat there by myself watching some horrible movie while the entire time I felt like an asshole. And now I have the mother of all stiff necks," I said.

"Is there anything else? Because the after-party is down the street and I want to get there before Kitty," Ms. D said.

"No, let's go," I said. "They better have muscle-relaxer mojitos there because I think I did some serious damage here."

"Okay, what is your problem?" Ms. D asked as we walked toward the nightclub. "This is more than a stiff neck."

"I met this guy," I began.

"Uh-huh. Of course you did."

"But once I told him that you and I weren't together, he wasn't into me at all. He only liked me when he thought I was straight."

"WHAT?" Ms. D gasped.

"I know, can you believe it?" I said. Out of habit, I tried shaking my head in shock. "OUCH!" I yelled.

"No, I mean I can't believe you told the publicist for the event that you and I weren't there together. Are you crazy?" Ms. D scolded.

"Oh, Jesus, do you really think anyone there thought that we were together? I'm obviously gay." I noticed Ms. D was weirdly silent. I turned my entire body and looked at her. She was on her phone texting. "Anyway, he'll be at the party. Hopefully, he'll realize what an ass he was being. I really felt something there. Do you think I still have a chance?"

"Um, Rob, I'm not sure I'm going to be able to get you into this party," Ms. D said as casually as if she had just told me she was out of gum.

"What? You can't tell me that they are going to give you shit for showing up with people to the after-party."

Silence.

"Oh, I get it. You gave my spot away to someone else and most likely one of their friends?" I said. "Let me guess, your seatmate during the movie?"

"I'm sorry, but we just met. You know how it is when you first meet someone and you think there's potential there. This could be the night I met the love of my life!" she said with a giant and playful smile. She draped her arm over my shoulder.

"If you touch my neck, I'm e-mailing Page Six about Kitty Meow," I said.

"So sensitive tonight," she said. "You're not even thirty yet. Come talk to me then about heartache." Ms. D kissed my cheek.

"You're really awful at cheering people up, you know that?" I smiled.

"Said the guy who was supposed to be cheering me up over *my* breakup."

"Let's call it a wash," I said.

We neared the nightclub and I walked Ms. D to the velvet ropes. Three people were waiting there to go inside with her. I looked at Ms. D again and noticed that standing behind her was the publicist from the earlier event. Ms. D noticed my eyes going off of her and onto him.

"Is that him?" she asked.

"That's the one," I said and smiled.

"Noted," she said. "I'll 'accidentally' spill a drink on him inside on your behalf."

"You're the best."

"Okay, I'll talk to you soon?" she said as her new love and his two friends formed a line behind her.

"Yes, I guess I'm leaving then?" I was actually relieved that I wasn't going inside. I had already embarrassed myself once that night and I wasn't about to do it again.

Ms. D went inside and I gave Ryan one last look before turning around and hailing a cab home.

I pulled out my phone. It was risky calling my mother so close to the ten o'clock cutoff, but this night was just too out of control not to tell her. Besides, I was too embarrassed to tell my other friends about it. They hated Ms. D. The entire conversation would be about how I was an idiot for going with her to a movie premiere in the first place. They were pretty much right, but that's not what I was looking to hear. I knew my mother would give me some sort of sage advice and encouraging words.

After hearing the full rundown of the evening, my annoyed mother said to me, "Look, kid, you need to decide if you're *in* or *out* and be happy with that. You know that better than anyone."

"Oh, come on, you don't think I was seriously going to go back into the closet for this guy, did you?" I shouted into my phone, startling the cab driver.

"Hello? Are you forgetting who you're talking to?" she asked.

"But . . ." I began.

"But what? It wouldn't be that big of a stretch for you to go back in the closet," she said.

The truth was my mom was always more reasonable than my father, or anyone in my immediate family for that matter. She doesn't make decisions on emotion or impulse.

"I know you're right. It's so strange to me though that someone would be so self-loathing that they were only interested in me if I was straight and had a girlfriend," I said as the taxi turned down my block.

"Of course, it's beyond weird. I'm sure you didn't expect this kind of reaction from someone amongst your own tribe, but I can assure you that creeps aren't simply relegated to gay or straight, they know no boundaries," she said.

"I guess you're right. But hey, for a second I was going to be Ms. D's new flavor of the moment, at least in photos. That's pretty cool, right? I was straight again even if it was only for a few minutes," I said.

"You were still gay. Good night, Robert."

"Fine. Good night."

Mama Says

The weekend after Robert's call I went to the hair salon. My hairdresser of the last six years was out sick one afternoon and, frankly, it was a gift from God. I had been trying to escape her for years, but every time I tried she would call me to remind me that I was due for a cut and color. That should have been my first red flag. What hairdresser calls the client to come in? Anyway, she called me one day coughing into the phone telling me that she was going to have to cancel my appointment because she had some sort of nasal infection. She asked to reschedule me the following week and was stunned when I told her that I needed to get in right away because I was leaving for New York in three days.

"I guess I could come in," she said, hacking into the phone.

"Uh, no, that's okay," I said. "I'll figure something out."

"Oh," she said, sounding disappointed.

"Listen, get some sleep and feel better. I'll speak to you soon," I said and quickly hung up the phone.

FREEDOM! I immediately took out the number of another salon that recently opened in town and made an appointment for the following day. The truth was that I really needed a good haircut and style since I was headed to New York to visit Robert. He'd invited me to attend an event he was putting on and the old lady 'do I was sporting wasn't working. I felt bad about divorcing my old hairdresser, but hey, breakups happen.

The next day I arrived at the salon for my appointment and was greeted by my new hairdresser, Peggy. I liked her almost immedi-ately. She was quirky and funny. She brought me to her chair and she told me what I needed to do with my hair—some blond high-lights and to go shorter. I already liked this woman better. She had a plan.

After I returned from the shampoo station, Peggy started to cut my hair. Since we didn't know each other, she made the obligatory hairdresser small talk. I didn't mind, especially with the excitement of being in a new place.

"So you said you're going on a trip. Where are you off to?" Peggy asked.

"I'm going to New York City to go to an event with my son," I said with a smile. One of the receptionists brought me a cappuccino. I loved this place.

Out of the clear blue, her cheerful smile turned to a look of disgust. *Had I done something wrong? Was I not supposed to take the cappuccino? Was this some kind of a trick?*

"New York? Hmph," she said, and rolled her eyes. "Are you go-ing to some gay thing?"

I must have looked like a deer in headlights. "What did you say?"

She repeated, "Are you going to some sort of gay thing?"

My immediate thought wasn't that she was being a total homo-phobe. Instead I thought that she was some sort of mind reader. I kept telling myself to clear my head in case she was. Unfortunately, I couldn't get the word "witch" out of my mind.

After realizing that she hadn't heard my inner witch comment, I took a deep breath and said, "Why would you say that?"

"I don't agree with homosexuality. I think it's a sick choice," she said as her cheerful tone turned frightening. Keep in mind this woman had scissors in her hand and was inches away from my throat. I wasn't sure what was going to happen next.

I felt my face getting redder by the minute. I could have stayed quiet and let her finish my hair. I could have simply shrugged my shoulders and thought to myself that it wasn't worth arguing with someone like Peggy who would obviously never get it. I could have done all of those things. But I didn't.

I felt a strange surge of adrenaline. "I feel it isn't a choice, but something genetic. And actually, Peggy, my son is gay."

"I don't agree with that lifestyle," Peggy said, with her hands gripping her scissors tightly.

I took a deep breath and made a choice. This could end in a shouting match or I could have a calm and rational conversation with her. "Well, it's not something you either agree or disagree with, it just is. Do you agree or disagree that I have blue eyes? No. The fact is I have blue eyes."

Peggy looked at me in the mirror and didn't say a word. I continued, "I understand and respect your feelings." I sat up in my chair and took a sip of my cappuccino to collect my thoughts. "Look at it this way. We live in a fairly small town, right?" I asked.

Peggy shrugged. "It's not that small."

"Right. But it's not as big as say Peoria or Chicago, correct?"

"Yes," she said.

"I'm not sure how old you are, but in the not-so-distant past people freaked out if they dated outside of their race. Think about it. What if your son or daughter came home with someone from another culture or even race back then?" I asked. "Or even now, for that matter? Racism still exists."

Before I could say another word, Peggy interrupted me. "I've been married to a black man for twenty-five years and we have two kids."

"Then you should know exactly what it's like to be stared at and judged unfairly. I'm sure there have been times over the years it's happened to you or God forbid even your children."

"Yes, it has," she said. "But this is different; homosexuality is a choice."

"I can tell you mother to mother, my son did not choose this."

"I'm sorry I can't agree with you," she said.

This went on for about another thirty minutes until finally we agreed to disagree. "I want to say one last thing. I love my son un-conditionally." I purposely didn't say "gay son" because "gay" is one one-thousandth of who Robert is. I love the gay part and I love everything else about him.

I'm not sure I convinced Peggy of much that afternoon, but she did listen to me. I could have walked out the minute she started up about not agreeing with the gay lifestyle, but where does that ever get anyone? If it takes one person at a time, then yes, sitting through an uncomfortable conversation is worth it. The reality is, the only way we are going to better understand each other is through a dia-logue. Sure, we might not always agree, but it takes courage and conviction to stand your ground and explain why.

So when Robert told me about what happened with the guy at the movie premiere, I simply told him not to doubt himself about coming out. He made the commitment to living an authentic life and he was finally happy. I could have kept quiet that day, but I didn't and neither should he. I said to him, "If you came out of the closet, don't I have to be ready to help you stay out? Be proud of who you are. Forget the closet, life is not a do-over."

And guess what? I still got a great haircut that day. So whether Peggy liked it or not, I looked pretty darn good for the "gay event" in New York, as she called it.

CHAPTER TWELVE
Faking It
___

I'm out, now what? Oh, pretend all of these
things make me happy. Riiiight.

After making it through the coming-out process relatively un-
scathed, I was ready to have some fun.

I was having a hard time getting over my shyness and meeting
other people during my first six months in New York. Then I met
Keith one day at my neighborhood gym. I'm fully aware that meeting
another gay guy at the gym sounds like a cliché, but hey, it was the
late nineties, I was twenty-two and very much a gay cliché, thank you
very much. Keith was the exact opposite of me. He was outgoing,
self-confident, blunt, and at times aggressive. He also asked me to go
home with him an hour after we met.

Despite his overly aggressive and voracious sexual appetite, his
many other personality traits made him exactly the kind of friend
I needed to raise my confidence level around other gays. He simply
didn't care what anyone thought of him. He wasn't afraid of being
rejected and his main goal was to have fun wherever he was. I, on
the other hand, overanalyzed everything and my own neurosis was
stunting any possibility for social growth. Keith was the other end
of the spectrum, but that's precisely what I needed. Otherwise I
was in serious danger of becoming a shut-in.

Keith and I both worked in publicity. However, our work ethic
was entirely different. I worked ten-hour days, ate my lunch at my
desk, and sometimes had to work weekends. He, on the other
hand, worked for a couple hours a day and had Fridays off in the
summer. The main differences between Keith and me were that he

was thirty-five and a vice president of public relations at a large company and I was twenty-two and an assistant at a small theater PR firm. Yet Keith ignored the great disparity between his job and mine. It didn't matter how tired I was when I got home, because Keith would show up at my building with a full itinerary for that evening. Typically, we would go downtown for dinner and drinks at whichever restaurant he was calling his favorite that particular week. Our dinner and drink combo nights usually ended up being marathons. They also ended up costing each of us around eighty bucks nearly every night or every other night. During the week we'd typically head back to the Upper West Side around one thirty or two in the morning. I had to be to work by eight thirty and Keith typically didn't stroll into work until somewhere in the vicinity of ten thirty or eleven o'clock, depending on how tired he was from the previous night. We were two single gay men enjoying everything that a city like New York had to offer, no matter what the price.

At around two in the afternoon on a Monday I received a forwarded e-mail from Keith inviting him and a guest to a birthday dinner Friday night in East Hampton with a note from Keith that read, "You MUST come."

I typed a one-word response and hit the send button.

The phone rang. "Oh my God!" he said.

"What?"

"What do you mean 'NO'? You have to go to John's birthday dinner this weekend. You're coming to East Hampton as my guest. What are you going to do? Stay home?"

"Um, that's exactly what I'm going to do. I can pick up some food at the market and drink an entire bottle of wine at the house, and it still won't be half of what I would end up spending at dinner," I said.

"He's going to be really upset if you don't go."

"I met him last weekend. He didn't invite me. Unless, that is, I introduced myself as 'guest' in a drunken haze. So, I don't think he invited *me*, Keith. Honestly, I'm not in the slightest bit concerned if he's upset or not. He's not paying my bills. And the only reason you're going to this fiesta is because you want to try and sleep with him."

Keith paused and then said, "That's not the point. You have to go."

John is the kind of guy who has to be the center of every story. When I met him the weekend before, there were six of us standing in a group at a bar and John had to be the master of ceremonies for everything. God forbid you interrupt him or speak to someone else while he's in the middle of one of his nonsensical stories or while he's quoting one of his favorite TV shows, *Designing Women*.

When John began quoting Suzanne Sugarbaker, I thought it was the perfect opportunity to turn to Keith to ask him about a guy I saw on the other side of the bar. The words had no sooner left my mouth before John scolded me. "Robert! You're missing the story. Listen!" Since I was the newest addition to this group of friends I felt doubly embarrassed. I felt like I was watching a petulant child screaming, "Watch me, guys! You're not watching. Come on, WATCH ME!" When I looked at Keith for help, he shrugged. Keith was buying anything that John was selling, at least until he slept with him. There was no way I was going to watch this play on a loop at dinner.

I opened my mouth in shock. "Um, sorry?" I said.

John glared at me and continued on. "Anyway, before I was rudely interrupted . . . Suzanne said, 'She said it was a gag gift.' And then Julia said, 'It certainly made me gag,'" he said, and then laughed hysterically at his own delivery. Everyone else joined in laughter, everyone except me. At that moment I actually did have something in common with Julia Sugarbaker; I also wanted to gag.

I wasn't about to waste a weekend and a good chunk of change on this nonsense.

"Wait, I just looked at my calendar. I can't go to East Hampton after all."

"Okay, here we go. I'll play along. Why, Robert?" he asked.

"I have to stay in the city this weekend and feed my neighbor's cat. Sorry."

"That's the best you can do? Try harder, young one. You don't talk to your neighbors and you hate cats," he said.

"I love all animals!" I shouted into the phone.

"Yes, but you're freaked out by cats. You already told me that. Come on, what else you got? You really need to try and be at least a little creative."

"How about this? This is NOT how I want to spend a hundred dollars," I said.

The weekend was already becoming more expensive than I wanted. I dropped $175 on a ticket to some dinner dance for charity that was the night after John's dinner. Keith insisted that I had to go because everyone would be there and it would be a great place for me to meet my new boyfriend or network for a new job. The reality was I didn't care so much about having a boyfriend or finding a new job, but I did like meeting new people and hopefully some of these new people would like to stay in on a Friday or Saturday night and hang out by doing something "cheap and cheerful." By this point it was the middle of the summer, and I was severely hemorrhaging money.

"Actually, it's going to be more like one fifty. I thought we could go in together on a birthday gift for John."

"A GIFT? Are you fucking kidding me? Why would I buy a total stranger a gift?"

"It's etiquette, Robert. Plain and simple. You're twenty-two, I know you're not versed in this yet, but thankfully you have me to teach you."

"Etiquette is not a problem for me, Keith. Finance, however, is. That's $325 spoken for before I even get on the Hampton Jitney."

"Oh, come on, it's only an extra fifty dollars. How many awful theater shows did I go see to support you?" he asked.

"Um, you got house seats for free to two Broadway shows, Keith. And you asked me for them."

"Irregardless, I want you to come. We'll have fun and plus we make good wingmen," he said.

"Okay, seriously, 'irregardless' is not a word. I've told you that over a hundred times and now you are starting to sound like an idiot. Secondly, Mr. Wingman, last weekend you disappeared from the bar without telling me."

"I woke up in the Bronx. I think you came out ahead in this situation," Keith said.

"Fine, I will go to the Hamptons and I will go to this stupid dinner, but I won't be happy about it," I said.

"Wow. I can't wait," Keith said. "You make it sound about as much fun as a root canal."

I ignored his comment and continued, "And if you sit me next to 'Au Naturel Andy' I will vomit into my napkin right there at the table."

"Au Naturel Andy" had been in East Hampton one of the previous weekends that I was there. I quickly learned that Andy didn't like anything that had to do with soap, deodorant, or colognes. This was now the second person I met who had an affinity for the natural sweat smell. I, on the other hand, liked to breathe without gagging.

"I will make sure you and I are sitting next to each other," Keith said.

"Keith, I'm serious. I can't handle that. He really smells like an old diaper."

"Okay, okay, I got it," he said. I thought I was about done with this train wreck of a conversation until Keith threw in one last thing. "Oh, I'm going to need you to leave the fifty bucks in an envelope with my doorman so I can get John's present."

I finally understood the allure of people like Naomi who throw their phones at their assistants, because if Keith had been in the room I would have broken mine on his forehead. He made six figures easily, and he was worried about fifty dollars.

"You're joking, right? You want me to leave money with your doorman?" I said.

"Hmm . . . Yeah, you're right, that may not be a good idea. Why don't you just go pick up something and I'll pay you back."

"Sure, that makes sense. I'll pick up a birthday present for a guy I barely know, but okay." I didn't know when I would have the time to leave work to go pick this gift up or where I would get the extra cash, but Keith didn't seem too concerned about it.

"Oh! By the way, I didn't want to mention it earlier, but we're not taking the Jitney. I thought it'd be better if we rented a car. But don't worry I'll get that money from you when we turn the car in."

I was silent. "Are you there?" Keith asked.

"Shh, I'm waiting to see if I can actually hear the brain aneurism explode in my head," I said.

"We're going to have so much fun this weekend!" Keith said.

"You're from hell," I said, and hung up the phone.

Thankfully, work was particularly slow that week and I managed to leave the office before seven. I was at a complete loss of what to buy for someone I barely knew. Obviously, I could go with clothes, cologne, or anything that I would want. I called Keith and he suggested that I pick something up from a store like Crate & Barrel. I was already downtown and had no interest in going back to Fifty-ninth and Madison during rush hour. I walked around for over an hour looking for something—anything—until I saw a fur-

niture store with a giant sign in the window that read, CHEAP CHAIRS
FOR YOUR CHEAP ASS.

Perfect.

A few days later Keith was outside of my building in the rental car.
I grabbed my bag and the meticulously wrapped birthday present.
When I got outside, Keith was waiting for me in a black Mercedes
SUV.

"This is our rental car?" I said.

"Don't you love it?" he said.

"Who else are we picking up?" I asked.

"No one. It's just us, why?"

"Because you rented an SUV. If we were taking three other
grown men or a litter of children, then and only then would I understand it."

"I think it's chic."

"I think I'm not paying for it."

"Oh lighten up, we're going to the Hamptons. We need something hot!"

"We took a bus last time," I said.

"Exactly," Keith scoffed.

The drive to the East End was excruciatingly longer than usual.
Friday afternoon traffic was unbearable and Keith refused to let me
nap. Instead, he told me all of the things he had booked for us for
the second half of the summer. It was like we were boyfriends without the sex. When Keith mentioned the remaining events on his
social calendar, I got a sharp pang in my stomach. My credit card
bill was going to be arriving any day and I knew it was going to be
bad. I hadn't paid the entire balance for the last two months.

When we arrived, Keith's friend Dean was already sitting in the
kitchen sipping on a cocktail. I instantly remembered why I liked
Dean. He was a silver fox; that is, he would be if he allowed his hair
to actually go gray. He was nearly twenty-five years older than me

and had a better body than me. He lifted up his shirt and asked me if I had an eight-pack like his yet. And then I remembered why I loathed Dean: He had a perfect body.

"I'll tell you what I don't have that you have," I said.

"What's that?" Dean asked.

"Age spots," I said as I hugged him hello.

"Nice Gucci sunglasses. Still only an assistant?" he said as he hugged me back. This was our relationship. Playful banter, yet with Dean I knew it wasn't coming from a mean place. I enjoyed it actually.

"I picked up tickets for us for some Hetrick-Martin benefit at some house on Lily Pond Lane," Dean said.

"Amazing," Keith said.

"Aren't we already going to a charity thing tomorrow night?" I asked.

"That's a different one," Dean answered.

"I'm going to need charity after all of this charity," I said. I was only half-joking.

"Then say no," Dean said. "Stay home."

"I know, but then I feel like I'm missing out or won't ever meet anyone," I argued.

"Then get another job, but stop complaining about it. You're twenty-two, not two," Dean said.

"Maybe I am acting like I'm two because like any good two-year-old, it's nap time and this kid's tired." I went into one of the back bedrooms and collapsed onto the bed, hoping that when I woke up my financial situation would be completely different and the American Express bill would magically disappear. I lay in bed and looked around the room. It was straight out of *Elle Décor*. I took a deep breath and wanted to cry. Even though I was surrounded by so many beautiful things, the reality was that I couldn't afford any of them. Dean's joke may have hit more of a nerve than I cared to realize. *Why couldn't I simply tell Keith no? What was I so afraid of? I wouldn't be invited to places anymore? I wouldn't have friends? At the rate I was spending, I wouldn't have a place to live in.* The fact was I was living a life that wasn't my own.

The Talking Heads song "Once in a Lifetime" popped into my head as I began to fall asleep. Before I drifted off I remember singing out loud, "You may ask yourself, where is that large automobile? You may tell yourself, this is not my beautiful house . . ."

At around eight thirty, Keith came into my room and turned on the light. "Hey, you might want to get ready. We're leaving here in twenty minutes. Dinner is at nine."

I lifted my head out of a deep sleep and tried to focus my eyes on Keith. I wasn't sure where I was. I was sleeping that soundly. After a minute or two, I finally said, "Okay, how much time do I have again?"

Keith looked at his watch and said, "Well, now you have seventeen minutes."

I sat up and said nothing. Keith stared at me, not sure what I was going to do next. I stood up and silently walked past him all the way to the kitchen. Keith trailed behind me and Dean quickly followed. I grabbed a 7-Eleven Big Gulp cup out of the cupboard and placed it on the counter. I opened the freezer and emptied an ice tray into the cup. I grabbed the vodka and began to pour without stopping.

"Are you going for a coma or death?" Dean asked. I turned my head toward Dean and without taking my eyes off of him, stopped pouring. I grabbed the soda and added a splash to my cup.

"I need to be severely loose if I'm going to sit through this dinner," I said, still groggy.

"How are you going to have time to drink that? We have to leave," Dean asked.

"Yeah, don't you have to get ready? We were at the beach all day. Aren't you at least going to shower?" Keith asked.

I looked at them both and very seriously said, "No. Let everyone think it's Au Naturel Andy."

"Oh, this is going to be an interesting night," Dean said.

I leaned against the counter and gulped my drink. I had no intention of finishing it, but I had every intention of making my point to Keith. Before I could take another sip, Keith ushered me into the bedroom to hurry and get dressed.

We walked into the restaurant and were the first to arrive. Dean sat next to Keith and when I went to pull out the chair on the other side of him, Keith quickly shooed me away from it. He was saving the seat for John so they could "bond."

"Where am I supposed to sit?" I asked.

"Sit across from us," Dean said. Luckily, I had those few sips of vodka before we left because otherwise I would have been extremely irritated by this. Instead, I went with the flow.

"Au Naturel Andy" arrived next with a very attractive date on his arm. He was tall with dark hair, brown eyes, and a sleeve of tattoos that emerged from his white Polo shirt. Andy introduced him to the table. His name was Lenny.

"Like Lenny and Squiggy from *Laverne & Shirley*?" I said, and smiled.

"No," he said, without smiling.

"Noted," I said.

It was safe to say that the vodka was already starting to course through my veins. When I moved in to shake Lenny's hand, I noticed that he too was not a fan of soap. In keeping with Murphy's Law, Andy and his date sat next to me. Thankfully, I had also opted out of a shower before arriving so I fit right in. I could barely contain my excitement about sitting next to the equivalent of two farting dogs when John walked into the restaurant.

"You guys brought a gift?" Andy asked before John got to the table. "That's so sweet."

"Didn't you?" I asked.

"No, we never do. We're already spending money on dinner and then plus a gift? It really adds up fast. John never buys birthday presents, either," Andy explained.

"Oh, okay. That makes sense," I said, and shot Keith a death stare.

"What's different about you?" Andy asked.

"Nothing since the last time that I saw you, I don't think," I said.

"Hmm, I don't know what it is, but I'll figure it out," Au Naturel Andy said, then squinted his eyes and looked me over again.

"Oh! I didn't shower. Maybe it's that? My pheromones are different!" Andy and Lenny turned their heads toward me in surprise.

"There's the birthday boy!" Keith said and stood up, saving everyone at the table from an awkward moment. He hugged and kissed John hello.

Keith was too busy fawning over John to notice that John was holding someone's hand. I, of course, seized on this opportunity. His date was maybe twenty-one. Maybe.

"Hi, I'm Robert," I said as I stood up and shook the guy's hand. Andy and Lenny remained seated. Dean stood to see what this young guy had to offer.

"Billy Jack, nice to meet you," he said and shook my hand.

"I'm sorry?" Dean asked.

"Billy Jack," he repeated.

"Jack is your last name?" Dean continued.

"No, it's my middle name. But I go by Billy Jack. Think Billy Ray Cyrus," he explained.

"I'd rather not," Dean said and took his seat. John and Billy Jack sat down. To Keith's horror, Billy Jack sat next to him and John sat next to me.

Thankfully, the waiter came by right at that moment so I wouldn't have to make uncomfortable conversation.

"How we doing here, folks? Can I get you started off with any drinks?"

"YES!" Dean and Keith said in unison.

Before anyone could place an order, John interrupted and said, "Actually, you know what? I think we'll get a couple bottles of wine for the table. Give us a good cab and for the white, maybe something a little fruity for this bunch," John said to the annoyed waiter.

When no one laughed, John said to the table, "Did you hear my joke? Something fruity for this bunch?" He laughed once again at his own joke. A few people gave a couple mercy laughs, but I was silent. John turned to his date and, as if on cue, he laughed and kissed John.

"Oh, I heard it. It just wasn't funny, as usual," I said under my breath.

Keith stepped on my toe under the table. I looked at him from across the table and shrugged. "I make a Lenny and Squiggy joke and I die a slow death. I don't get it."

We made polite conversation until the waiter came back with the two bottles of wine. I stuck a large piece of bread in my mouth so I didn't say anything else to further embarrass myself. The waiter poured us all a glass and like clockwork, John stood up to make a toast.

"I'm so happy to be celebrating my birthday with my boys!" John said and looked around the table. "I couldn't have asked for a better group of guys."

I found this incredibly alarming as I'd only been around John twice before and Billy Jack seemed fairly new to the equation, too, but I went along with it and raised my glass to toast John. I realized that I could very well be him if I continued on the same path.

The next two hours were filled with enough quotes from *Designing Women*, *Maude*, *The Golden Girls*, and *Absolutely Fabulous* that I was ready to vomit glitter.

"Did I see a big, shiny present with my name on it when I walked in?" John said with a definite slur.

"Yes!" Keith said, especially excited. "I couldn't not get you something."

The rest of the table looked at one another and collectively rolled our eyes. "Should we wait for the birthday cake and then I'll open the present?" John asked. Once again, the table looked at each other, bewildered. Nobody got a cake.

"Honey, we didn't get you a cake because we knew you were trying to maintain that gorgeous body of yours," Dean said, covering.

"You guys are the best," John said.

I would have been devastated without a cake. As a former fat kid, birthday cake is the only reason for birthdays. If my friends didn't get me a cake, they might as well be dead to me.

"So open your present!" Keith said. I wasn't sure where Keith's excitement about the gift was coming from since he didn't even know what was inside.

"Cool it, Keith. He'll open it when he's ready," I said. Keith ignored me and grabbed the present off the ground and handed it to John.

"You really didn't have to get me anything," John said.

"I wanted to," Keith said, trying his best to move in on Billy Jack's territory.

John unwrapped his present in record time and had a confused look on his face.

"What is it?" Lenny asked.

"Yeah, what is it, John?" Andy said.

"It's a metal frog," John said.

"It's not just a metal frog, John, it's a watering can to water your flowers and plants. Oh! And there's this little compartment inside that you can use to hide your house key in case you're ever locked out," I explained. Keith's face turned as green as the frog.

John pulled it out of the box and set it in the center of the table, where it was met with smiles and laughter. I thought it was perfect. Keith, however, did not.

"Let me see that!" Billy Jack said excitedly. "It's so cool! You can leave this out in your kitchen, babe."

"Keith, I really don't know what to say. Really, I don't," John said.

Keith smiled and looked at me and then back at John. "That's not your real present. It's a joke," Keith said and faked a laugh.

"It is?" John said, relieved.

"It is?" I repeated.

"I bought you a ticket for the dinner and dance tomorrow night at the airport hangar," Keith said.

"That is so sweet of you! We weren't going to go because I only had one ticket, but now Billy Jack can use mine and I'll use my gift from you. You're the best," John said and kissed Keith on the cheek.

Billy Jack came over to John and kissed him. The two then became mesmerized by the frog and Keith took that as his cue to come and berate me about the gift.

"Are you kidding me? That better not have cost a hundred dollars," Keith said in a huff.

"No! I bought it on sale for eleven. Can you believe it?"

"Where did you get this, Jennifer Convertibles?" Keith hissed.

"Of course not!" I said. "They were closed. I found it at this little store on Seventh Avenue South," I said and smiled.

"You're such an ass," Keith said.

"Keith, I sincerely thought it was a cute, fun gift. Why would I give someone I don't know a serious gift? That's ridiculous."

"You're ridiculous," he said as he watched the new couple play with their frog. "And by the way, you're giving John your ticket for his real birthday gift since you screwed this up."

"Great!" I said.

"For free!" he quickly said.

"Oh."

"We're not going tomorrow night. You can hang with us if you want," Au Naturel Andy said.

"Thanks, Andy," I said. The truth was that I didn't really want to go to some silly dinner and dance where I would be the youngest and the one with the smallest income. Plus, I knew that I wouldn't have to shower again if I hung out with Andy and Lenny.

"I brought the first season of *Absolutely Fabulous* with me," Lenny said excitedly.

"You rock, Squiggy," I lied. Lenny and Andy shot me another pissed look. "Still not funny? Really?" I asked.

The rest of the weekend was relatively quiet, yet still expensive since I had to cough up my ticket to John. I ended up spending money on a bottle of wine and snacks to bring over to Andy and Lenny's house. We had a blast playing board games, eating, and drinking wine. I even became immune to their scent, at least until I hugged them good-bye.

Before I knew it Keith and I were headed back to Manhattan in our rented luxury SUV. The closer we got to the city, the more I began to panic inside. I knew that my financial reality was going to be most likely waiting for me in the mail. I felt like someone was jumping up and down on my chest and, thanks to our late departure, we would have to pay for an additional day before returning the car.

Sunday evening at around eleven o'clock I finally walked into my apartment. I threw my keys and the weekend's unopened mail onto my coffee table and collapsed into my couch. I was completely exhausted. I didn't turn on the television, music, or even my computer. I sat and absorbed the silence. On the one hand it was amazing to have the stillness, but on the other hand I missed having other people around. As much as Keith grated on my nerves from time to time, he did make me laugh and made sure that I didn't sit in my house alone. I stretched and stared out my window. Then my damn inner voice started in on me. It shouted, "You don't have the money for any of this." It was followed by several choruses of "none of this is real" and "this is a life that you can't afford." It was everything that I was trying to drown out with dinners, events, parties, and weekend trips. Ironically, none of the "things" brought me any sort of joy, but the sense of being around a group of friends did. I believe I was trying to create a sort of family in New York, since I missed the one I left back home. I'm aware that it sounds like fucked-up logic, but I was twenty-two. My best friend, Marc, called it "rich people's problems." But I wasn't rich.

Finally, I sat up and grabbed the AmEx bill from under the pile of mail. I took a deep breath and held it in my hand for what seemed like hours before I ripped the corner off and pulled out the bill. I closed my eyes before looking at the balance. I said a prayer and hoped for the best. I opened my eyes and looked at the amount due.

$22,846.73.

I blame the metal frog for putting me over the top.

Mama Says

"Are you drunk?" I asked.

"Mom, it's eight in the morning," Robert said.

"You're twenty-two and living in New York. Well, are you?"

"What?"

"Drunk?" I repeated.

"NO!" he said.

"Twenty-two thousand dollars?" I said out loud. It was just too big of a number. What the hell could he have spent so much money on? "YOU'VE GOT TO BE KIDDING ME!" I said as it finally registered.

"I know," he said softly.

"Is this one of your jokes?" I asked. "Is your sister in on this?" It wouldn't have surprised me if Robert and his sister, Julie, had contrived this entire story just to get me worked up. Anything was possible when the two of them got together.

"In on what? I'm not joking. I owe twenty-two, almost twenty-three thousand dollars on my American Express card," he said. I could tell by the tone in his voice that he was gravely serious.

"How does that happen? American Express makes you pay it all at once," I said.

"I know. I've been paying a little bit at a time to keep them off my back," he explained. "I begged them not to cut it off and said that I'd have the money to them by the end of this month. I didn't realize that with interest and everything that it got this out of hand."

139

"What did you spend all of this money on? Are you on drugs? Are you supporting someone else? What is going on out there?"

"I don't know. I got caught up. Charity events, dinners, gym memberships, lunches, clothes, weekend trips, you name it."

"That is insanity. Pure insanity," I said. "Seriously? Who do you think you are? You're not from one of those New York society families."

"Trust me, I know. I feel horrible about it. Disgusting, actually."

"I-I-I don't even know what to say," I said. "You're twenty-two. I don't know any other twenty-two-year-olds who spend like this. I've heard of getting out of hand with credit cards by spending maybe a couple hundred bucks, or maybe even a thousand, but you took this to an entirely new stratosphere."

By this point my reality had become completely distorted. I didn't know what was real and what wasn't. I know Robert is responsible. I know he has a good head on his shoulders. How did this happen? My head was swirling.

Then a switch went off inside me and I flashed to standing at our neighborhood park with Mike, Julie, and Robert when they were little. I had gotten into a similar situation nearly twenty years ago.

The park was packed with mothers in the morning looking on as their kids played. I usually sat at a picnic table and watched as my oldest son played sports with the other boys and my daughter tried her best to join them. I had to pay close attention to Robert as he was usually trying to eat dirt in the sandbox.

The truth of the matter was that I wanted my kids to have things and experiences and if that meant less for me, I honestly didn't care. Their happiness was more important. I thought I released all of those wants until one day when I was watching the kids play and two women came over and sat down at the table. I'd seen them at the park several times before and always smiled politely, but they never really talked with me.

One of them was going on and on about her new diamond tennis bracelet and the other was showing off her purse that she bought for herself the day before. The brunette asked how I was able to keep everything together in my purse since it was so worn and did I worry that things would fall out? I knew she wasn't actually concerned. She was simply being mean. The blonde made a joke, asking why I didn't just use a grocery bag instead.

I was in high school all over again.

With a first name like Jane, you'd think I'd be ready to let it go. Don't get me wrong, I love my name. But after growing up being called *Plain Jane* by a bunch of schoolyard kids, I began to hate it. What's worse is that I started to view myself as exactly that . . . a plain Jane. No matter how pretty a sweater I was wearing, or how much time I'd spent on my hair and makeup, I always felt the sting of "plain Jane" when I looked in the mirror before going to school.

I finally said *hasta la vista* to my classmates who christened me with a nickname I hated, and I said *hello, baby* to my son Michael, then Julie, and eventually Robert. But even after all the years of focusing on my kids, something bizarre was triggered inside me that day on the playground.

I was Plain Jane again.

But this time I was going to rewrite the script. I was going to change things up in a very big way. A week later, I went to our local department store and bought a beautiful designer purse. I didn't have that kind of cash lying around, so I put it on my credit card. I felt guilty while buying it and even more guilty for not telling my husband. I felt like he wouldn't understand. I went to the park the next day and sat at the same table while the kids played. Like clockwork, the same catty women strolled up to the table.

"Whose purse is that?" the blonde said.

"I wonder if someone left it there," the brunette said.

"It's mine," I said proudly. The two women looked at me strangely.

"Yours?" the blonde asked.

"Yes, mine," I said and turned back around to watch the kids.

"It's gorgeous," the brunette said.

"Thanks," I said without turning back around.

The validation was a rush of adrenaline to me and very soon I was showing up to the park dressed like I was going to Sunday brunch or a business meeting. I bought new clothes, jewelry, shoes, and watches. This wasn't me at all. These women were nearly ten years older than I was since I was a young mom, but for whatever reason I still needed their validation. I'll be honest: I felt inferior and I was insecure.

Ron asked where all of this new stuff was coming from and I found myself telling him that it was old and that I hadn't brought it out in a while. I felt horrible about it, but it's amazing what we'll do to make people think we're as good as they are. It sounds like madness now, but then it seemed completely justifiable. Since I had married so young and had been raising kids most of my life, I had never joined the workforce. Therefore, I never had money of my own to spend. I completely understood the lure and seduction of the almighty credit card.

I quickly found myself buying things that I neither needed nor particularly liked in an effort to please the playground moms. It's something so many of us go through, whether gay or straight. We want to feel validated by everyone around us to the point where we lose ourselves somewhere in the process. I finally had to tell Ron when the credit card bill came. It was excessive, but nowhere near what Robert had spent. I knew Ron hated credit cards, and I shed a lot of tears when I told him. His philosophy was, "If you don't have the money to pay cash for something, you have no business buying it." We had to budget for the next several months to pay off the credit card but I learned my lesson. Thankfully, I learned it fairly early in life because the consequence of continuing to seek out this type of validation can hinder a person from developing a sense of one's self.

Mom," Robert said, snapping me out of my memory.

"We'll figure something out. I have some money in savings. I'll pay off the credit card."

"Oh my God. Thank you," Robert said.

I could tell that he was crying. It made no sense to make him feel any worse than he felt at that moment. "But you are going to pay me back."

"Of course. I'll pay you back a little bit every week."

"Yes, you will," I said.

"Thank you," he said. "I love you."

"I love you, too," I said.

"All right, I have to get to work," he said.

"Yes, you do. That's the only way I'm going to get paid back, so don't screw it up," I said and laughed. It felt good to break the tension.

Robert wasn't sure whether or not it was okay to laugh. "Um, I won't?"

"Oh, take a breath, Robert. It's going to be all right," I said.

"Thanks, Mom," he said.

"OH! Don't mention a word of this to your father," I said.

"Trust me, I won't," he said, and hung up the phone.

PART THREE:

The Dating Game

CHAPTER THIRTEEN

The Gay Glossary

Knowledge is power, especially when it comes to the double meanings of the gay lexicon. See also *bossy bottom*.

My older brother and sister grew up in a very different household than me. My parents were no-nonsense kind of people when it came to the rules of the house.

1. *No phone calls after 9 P.M.*

    THEM: It didn't matter if they were in mid-conversation or if it was nine o'clock and six seconds. My father would pull the plug from the wall.

    ME: If it was past nine, that usually meant my mom was watching Lifetime and my dad was asleep on the couch. I'd stay on the phone until around eleven, watch a little "skina-max," and then go to bed with them being none the wiser.

2. *Absolutely no swearing, or "cussing" as my parents called it.*

    THEM: If my brother or sister were having a bad day and words like "shit" or "damn" slipped out, they'd get their mouths washed out with soap.

    ME: At eleven years old, I was damning my shit-for-brains math teachers. Depending on their mood, my parents either laughed or told me to "watch my mouth," a phrase that was repeated to me for most of my adolescent life. More importantly, my mouth never touched a bar of Irish Spring.

3. *No R-rated movies until you're seventeen.*

THEM: My brother and sister pleaded to go with their friends to an "R" flick. My parents deemed them dirty.

ME: I saw *Porky's* when I was eight. My parents thought it was funny that I was so interested in women's breasts. I was known as the "boobman" from that point on. The nickname would be dropped only after I told them I was gay. The boobman wasn't a total lie. I was and still am fascinated by women's breasts, just not in that way.

4. *Absolutely no drinking or smoking.*

THEM: A rule my sister paid little attention to, as she puked all over her high school principal's shoes at a dance that my parents chaperoned. The following weekend, she passed my mother in her car smoking a cigarette while she was supposed to be in her third-hour English course. (My sister is now a tough-as-nails schoolteacher—go figure.)

ME: By the time I became a teenager (a full four years after my sister and nearly six after my brother), my parents had definitely loosened up. They hadn't exactly abandoned the drinking rules, but they were much more laid-back about them. I had glasses of wine with them every now and then, but to be honest I never really got drunk in high school, because seeing my sister get punished scared the hell out of me. In fact, my parents were almost worried that I wasn't getting drunk in high school. I felt peer pressure from them to drink!

My brother and sister are mortified to this day by the way I speak to my parents. What's more surprising is the fact that it's rubbed off on my parents. My mother recently got a bad haircut and told my brother she felt like a dyke with bad hair. My brother was aghast.

Apparently, not everything should be shared so openly. When my parents and I play cards (a tradition from an early age), we often refer to each other by our card-playing names. I'm "Asshole," my mother's "Stinky Bitch," and my father's "Fucking Prick."

Words are the great connectors in this world, and nothing could be truer when my mother called me one morning to show me just how much our lexicons differed. She had dropped three sizes thanks to the points. She had just returned from her morning meeting, where she had been rewarded with a congratulatory pin. "A pin?" she said in a huff. "Why would I want a pin announcing to the world that I was fatter than I am now? It's like asking a schizophrenic to wear a pin around town that says, 'Former Crazy!'

"Diane asked how your progress was coming along," she said. "I told her you were doing just great and that you were getting lots of looks lately. She thinks you are so cute and said it's fantastic you're gay," she added.

"That's because she's a fag hag," I shot back.

"Fag bag? Huh? What does that mean?" my mother asked, horrified. "By the way, I don't like that word fag, you know. It's degrading."

"Sorry, I didn't mean it to be, but since I'm gay, I can say it. I can take ownership of it," I replied. "Anyway, a fag *hag* is a woman who uses gay men as an emotional crutch when she can't find love and happiness of her own," I explained.

That gave me a genius idea. I decided to give my mother a pop quiz of commonly used gay words and phrases to see if she knew what they meant. It affectionately became known as the "gay glossary" in our house. It was no different from any foreign language translation guide one might take when traveling abroad and was just as vital when visiting your gay child or having a conversation with him via instant messenger. It was referenced often and updated almost weekly.

Since it was for my mother, I kept it fairly clean, but at the same time I wanted her to know what I was talking about when we had our conversations. "Why do you need your own language to be gay?" she asked in the beginning. Within a few months, my mother, in our small Illinois town, would meet friends at lunch and say things like, "Oh, quit being such a fag hag, Kathy. Everybody knows Peter's a queen and she's just his beard. I bet he's one of those bossy-bottom fellas, too. Those queens on the DL are the worst." Her friends often stared at her blankly, but soon our gay glossary had spilled into social circles where it was never meant to go.

We've included a small portion of it here.

6"
MOM'S DEFINITION: Oh God, Robert. I don't want to go there.
ACTUAL GAY DEFINITION: the average-sized male penis, a.k.a. 8" in most gay hook-up sites

6-pack
MOM'S DEFINITION: Beer? No, of course I know this, but those kinds of abs are strictly fantasy.
ACTUAL GAY DEFINITION: the prerequisite in finding a mate

A-gay
MOM'S DEFINITION: refers to gay people as in "my son is a gay"
ACTUAL GAY DEFINITION: the homosexual elite that have power, money, and privilege ("I will never be an A-gay.")

B&D
MOM'S DEFINITION: big and dumb
ACTUAL GAY DEFINITION: bondage and discipline; sexual activity related to being bound

bareback

MOM'S DEFINITION: looks good in a swimsuit!

ACTUAL GAY DEFINITION: sex without condoms, a.k.a. SUICIDE! Practice safe sex!

battle-ax

MOM'S DEFINITION: bitchy

ACTUAL GAY DEFINITION: an aggressive, ugly, or militant woman (or, as my mother said, a real bitch!)

bear

MOM'S DEFINITION: big

ACTUAL GAY DEFINITION: a hairy man of large stature, usually found in Vermont

Blanche

MOM'S DEFINITION: free stuff

ACTUAL GAY DEFINITION: refers to the promiscuous '80s sitcom *Golden Girls* character, Blanche Deveraux ("Oh, Blanche, your legs are open like an all-night diner, 24/7.")

BOB

MOM'S DEFINITION: Bring your own bottle. Cosmos, anyone?

ACTUAL GAY DEFINITION: battery-operated boyfriend

bossy bottom

MOM'S DEFINITION: a big butt

ACTUAL GAY DEFINITION: a person giving orders during sex, also known as "backseat driving"

breky

MOM'S DEFINITION: a person who breaks up a lot

ACTUAL GAY DEFINITION: breakfast

buff
MOM'S DEFINITION: nude
ACTUAL GAY DEFINITION: great body/muscular

Chelsea boy
MOM'S DEFINITION: a person who lives in that neighborhood and dates older men
ACTUAL GAY DEFINITION: *How did she know that they date older men?*

Cinderella fella
MOM'S DEFINITION: pretty boy
ACTUAL GAY DEFINITION: HOOKER!

circuit party
MOM'S DEFINITION: a place to meet other gay people
ACTUAL GAY DEFINITION: over!

DL
MOM'S DEFINITION: deep love for someone
ACTUAL GAY DEFINITION: the down-low; maintaining a public appearance of being straight

DQ
MOM'S DEFINITION: Dairy Queen?
ACTUAL GAY DEFINITION: drag queen

fierce
MOM'S DEFINITION: mean
ACTUAL GAY DEFINITION: adjective commonly used by queens and Chelsea boys; mind-blowing, strong

flagger
MOM'S DEFINITION: someone in a gang or rough around the edges

ACTUAL GAY DEFINITION: someone in the middle of a nightclub or party who starts twirling flags around; ANNOYING!

flame
MOM'S DEFINITION: girlish
ACTUAL GAY DEFINITION: TOTAL GIRL!

friend of Dorothy
MOM'S DEFINITION: a munchkin/a very small person
ACTUAL GAY DEFINITION: from gay icon Judy Garland, who acted as Dorothy in the film *The Wizard of Oz*; a homosexual

gaydar
MOM'S DEFINITION: able to find other guys right away
ACTUAL GAY DEFINITION: a kind of presumed instinct that seemingly enables gay people to ascertain that another person is gay (Something I was never born with, as I think everyone is straight.)

gym rat
MOM'S DEFINITION: guys that go to the gym for reasons other than to lift weights
ACTUAL GAY DEFINITION: a guy who spends most of his time in the gym, working out and improving his already great figure, but still acts like a big girl

leather daddy
MOM'S DEFINITION: a man who likes to wear a lot of leather
ACTUAL GAY DEFINITION: an older man dressed in leather who is the object of a younger man's affection, the latter usually dressed in a collar and/or harness

lipstick lesbian
MOM'S DEFINITION: a man who is gay and wants to be a woman lesbian
ACTUAL GAY DEFINITION: a lesbian who prefers to wear makeup and look conventionally feminine, as opposed to the BODs (big ole dykes)

mangina
MOM'S DEFINITION: an attractive gay man
ACTUAL GAY DEFINITION: a very fem guy (man + vagina) ("He's the biggest girl. He's a total mangina.")

metrosexual
MOM'S DEFINITION: straight men who pick up gays on the metro line
ACTUAL GAY DEFINITION: one beer away from gay

Miss thang
MOM'S DEFINITION: smart-ass
ACTUAL GAY DEFINITION: a cocky drag queen with lots of attitude

pig
MOM'S DEFINITION: fat
ACTUAL GAY DEFINITION: someone with an insatiable sexual appetite

PNP
MOM'S DEFINITION: to pick someone up
ACTUAL GAY DEFINITION: party and play, to pick someone up and do lots of drugs

queen
MOM'S DEFINITION: feminine-like
ACTUAL GAY DEFINITION: a man that acts like a big ole girl

theater queen
MOM'S DEFINITION: chorus boy on Broadway
ACTUAL GAY DEFINITION: a gay man devoted to
musical theater

tranny
MOM'S DEFINITION: transvestites that she sees in the
early morning walking near Robert's apartment in the
Meatpacking District
ACTUAL GAY DEFINITION: BINGO!

trick
MOM'S DEFINITION: a hooker
ACTUAL GAY DEFINITION: a one-night stand

U-Haul
MOM'S DEFINITION: a guy who pays for sex
ACTUAL GAY DEFINITION: what a lesbian brings on
her second date

Mama Says

When Robert and I were on the phone one day, he referenced the word "queen" in relation to a guy he knew. I didn't get it, but I let it go until he used it over and over again.

"I have no idea what you're saying," I told him.

"Oh, sorry. 'Queen' has a lot of meanings. Usually it's in reference to another gay guy, and can be used positively or negatively."

"I don't get it, but then again, I'm not meant to," I said.

He then started asking me a series of questions about different gay phrases and if I knew their meaning. I told him maybe I did, but why did I need to know? I'm all for understanding everything that involves my kids, but maybe there are some things I don't need to know.

However, he wasn't having any of it and thought it would be fun to quiz me. If you haven't already figured it out by now, I am up for almost anything and if it helps me better understand what's happening in the gay world, let's do it. Yet when we reached one of the questions—what does BOB mean?—and when he told me, "battery-operated boyfriend," I thought this was way too much information coming from my son. I didn't need to know that one. He couldn't stop laughing. I'm super open, but there're just some things I don't need to talk with my son about.

I cut him off after a few more terms.

"Okay, no more," I said.

"Come on, Mom, this is hilarious," he said laughing.

"I think this is one of those instances where if I don't ask, you don't tell me," I said, and then laughed.

CHAPTER FOURTEEN

Me, But Latin

The phrase most commonly uttered by gay men when asked what they are looking for in a potential mate

---

I graduated with my B.A. in Liberal Arts from what was touted in many magazines as the "Harvard of the Midwest," Illinois Wesleyan University, and within months, I left the Midwest behind and moved to New York. In a city that roared with noises of taxis, ambulance sirens, and airplanes, the silence in response to my résumé was deafening. (Unbeknownst to me, there were lots of young Midwesterners who had gone to the *real* Harvard looking for brighter days in the city as well.) I took my first job at a theater PR firm. I don't know if you could even call it a job, as I was a paid intern. An intern for what? I often wondered. It wasn't as if I needed college credit. I later realized that this "internship" was a way for my boss to justify paying me roughly two hundred dollars a week and soliciting my gratitude daily for the learning experience. I definitely learned a lot, but feeling thankful was a stretch. I would have been thankful if he had paid me enough to pay my rent or even buy groceries. As it was, I could afford less than half my rent each month.

The irony of me working at a theater PR firm was that I was part of a new generation of gay men who weren't enthralled with everything theater like the show tune–singing, *Cabaret*-quoting, piano bar–loving gay men before us. In fact, I found a lot of theater to be on the boring side. Therefore, finding a potential mate at any work-related function was impossible, because the minute the discussion turned to theater, I mentally checked out. Here I was, a closet writer, and I was dissing the theater. I felt like Judas.

I was fortunately blessed with parents who could pay for my college education. They unfortunately were blessed with a son who found a job that paid nil. Each month I'd have to make that embarrassing phone call home, begging for money. ("Change? Anyone got some change here?") I finally convinced them to think of it as if I were in graduate school and they were just paying for a further extension of my educational experience. They didn't necessarily buy my line of bullshit, but they did reward me for my creativity.

This arrangement worked out well, or so I thought. Things took a sharp turn when I put my weekly salary toward "entertainment expenses," which included dinners, drinking, and occasional trips to Barney's, leaving me with no money to pay my share of the bills. I was quickly urged to get a second job. So I did what any logical person would do: I enrolled in bartending school for $250, courtesy of my parents.

I found an ad for the classes in the back of the *Village Voice*. "Bartending Academy," it said. "Wow," I thought. "An academy!" I imagined an Ivy League–style place where men walked around with embroidered martini glass crests on their white dinner jackets and where the women, dressed in little black cocktail dresses, nodded knowingly at one another.

I walked up the six flights of steps in the run-down office building near Madison Square Garden. It smelled like my old fraternity, a combination of pee-stained floors, sweat, and stale beer. I entered the large classroom and saw a roomful of disgruntled men and women already standing behind their bars inspecting the equipment.

I debated throwing myself down the stairs, yet my strange fascination with bars and bar equipment as a kid drew me inside. I pulled some cologne out of my backpack and sprayed it on my arm to mask the building's stench. I figured that if the smell got too bad, I could always smell my arm for a temporary reprieve.

Harry, our teacher, stood five foot four, weighed about 175

pounds, and was pretty much a professional drunk. His permed hair was so tight that it actually looked like he had pubic hair on his head. It was only overshadowed by his thick mustache, which was discolored due to years of smoking. During his introductory speech, I realized that it wasn't the building that smelled—it was him.

Most of the people in the class were about my age, and they all had that blank gaze, dreaming of better days. A week later, the blank gaze had turned to a bitter stare. I was devoid of all emotion. I looked at it as I had most of my prior encounters with men: Get in, do your business, and get out. Finally, during week two, like a heavenly ray of light, in walked Brett, a guy that went to my gym who I'd been secretly obsessing over for nearly a year.

Harry didn't share my enthusiasm and growled at him to take the station next to mine. Luckily, Brenda, my previous partner, had been arrested for buying a dime bag in Washington Square Park the weekend before. Harry told Brett that he needed to stay after class to catch up to everyone else. Seeing this as my golden moment, I offered my exceptional bartending services (and any other services should he need them). However, as with most of my college books, I hadn't read a page of the manual.

Class ended at around eight thirty and I was brave enough to muster up the courage to speak.

"Hi there," I said nervously. He smiled and nodded while looking right through me. I knew this wasn't a good sign, but I was there to help and couldn't just slither away quietly.

"I think you work out at my gym," I said.

"Yeah. Could be," he said with disinterest.

"Yeah. In fact, you said what's up to me about five weeks ago," I confessed. Suddenly I had become a bad after-school special. He nodded again. Maybe he didn't understand. Maybe he was foreign? It was New York, after all. I kept at it. "Are you having fun?" I asked, showing him the proper four count of pouring alcohol into the glass.

"Not really. Not a lot of cute guys in this class," he said, pouring the faux vodka. He was completely off with his count, but who was I to judge such a beauty? I felt a burning in my throat. "Yeah, I guess you're right. What kind of guys do you like?" I heard myself ask, yet at the same time I couldn't believe I was actually pursuing it. Clearly, he couldn't have cared less if I stood in front of him and lit myself on fire.

He took a long pause, as if giving careful thought to my question, almost as if I'd asked what his views were on the U.S. welfare system.

"Well, I guess I like someone who's exactly like me—but Latin."

I cocked my head to the side like a confused dog and quickly scooted away without saying another word. I'd never before heard someone be so brazen about what they were looking for in a person. It's one thing to think it or reflect on it in a therapy session, but to actually be so direct dumbfounded me. I could barely finish my lesson on preparing a proper mint julep.

While I was walking home utterly depressed and slightly drunk, I realized that this had to be the reason I wasn't meeting anyone. I was too *white* for the gay community. I needed to invent a Latin heritage and fast if I ever wanted to have a boyfriend.

Do we have any Latin blood in our family?" I asked anxiously.

"What?" Mom said, shocked. I sat at the computer trying to find any Latin ties to my last name.

"Do we have any Latino heritage?" I repeated.

"Robert, look in the mirror, for God's sake! Do you think you look Latin?"

"Our last name sounds so generic. Something could've been dropped," I argued. Ever since I had left Illinois, everyone had commented on what a great name I had, although it was usually followed with the question I loathed: "Is that your real name?" People who aren't from the Midwest don't get that you don't just change your last name there. It's against their whole belief system. After I tell people this, they usually ask if I've shortened the name. No one will just accept that Rave is, in fact, my real last name. It sounds as generic as Smith or Jones, but for the good or the bad, it's mine. Up until then, I was happy with it. However, at that moment I was considering adding a "z" or an "o" to the end to give it some flava!

"I got news for you: It's your name, and as far as I know there's no Latin lineage to it. Honestly, I don't have time for this. I'm trying to pick out clothes for your dad's trip to the Kentucky Derby, since he can't pick out his own clothes," she said, hanging up the phone. (When my dad married my mom, he lost any ability he had to function without her, which is endearing to us kids but which dances on my mother's last nerve.)

I ignored her disparaging comments about my potential Latin heritage. She obviously didn't realize that if I was to find a date in this town, I needed some Latin blood and fast! I continued my Internet search. The news was heartbreaking. The name had roots in Austria and . . . oh, God . . . Germany, the whitest place on earth. Shit.

I quickly phoned my mother back. "What about your maiden name?"

"Norwegian and English." She slammed down the phone again. I wasn't sure if I totally believed her, as she was in the throes of matching pants and polo shirts, so I looked it up online. Sure enough, it was a name of English descent with most of my ancestors settling in Norway. I wasn't convinced. I had to have some type of Latin heritage in me somewhere. I was dedicated to finding it to make my move on Brett. He'd find out and then realize that I truly was him, only Latin. Well, almost.

I went to the New York Public Library to use their resources. This was my first and only time in the New York Public Library, I'm embarrassed to admit. Everything that I'd learned in high school and even at college about the U.S. library system totally left my brain the minute I received my degree. I quickly enlisted the help of Penny, a cute part-time librarian, to find my Latin roots.

She took me through stacks of books, written by people like Vonnegut, Steinbeck, Hemingway, and Shakespeare. None of them interested me. We finally reached a small section with books on genealogy. Penny thought her mission was complete. "Could you help me find my last name?" I begged. I turned on some straight-boy charm and inched closer to her, smiling. Instead, she read my charm as stupidity, as evidenced from her continuous eye rolling.

"Rave. Here it is," she said. I perused it quickly as Penny took her leave.

"Damn it," I yelled.

She turned back. "What's the problem?"

"Not a Latin thing in there," I huffed.

"What? You're joking, right?"

"No," I insisted. "I wish I were joking. Now I'm going to be single for life."

After several confused looks, I finally owned up to my real motive for being at the New York Public Library.

"That's repulsive. People have tried for years to assimilate into a white culture and erase their heritage, all in order to fit in with the white man and play by his rules, and here you are, a white man, who has lived with the privilege of being a white man his entire life, but that's not enough for you. Instead, you need to steal from the Latin people and 'fake it' as one of them." She rolled her eyes one last time and left me in the dark corner of the library with a stack of old books.

I was about to leave when I took one final glance down at the book and saw that in the 1800s, some of the Raves broke off and moved to the northern part of Spain. *Viva la Espanola!*

I showed up the following Tuesday for class with a certain swagger. It was obvious enough that even Harry stopped picking food out of his mustache long enough to notice. "Looks like somebody got lucky with the ladies," he said, giggling.

I continued my swagger and went to set up my bar. Brett was already at his station practicing. "Hi," I said confidently.

"'Sup?" he said, looking through me once again.

"Oh, nothing," I said. "I was home trying to plan a trip to visit my distant relatives in Spain," I said, beaming.

"Spain? That's cool, man," he said, pouring his vermouth.

"Did I tell you I was Latin?" I pushed.

"No," he said, uninterested. "You don't look it. You're blond."

"Yeah, I am. Totally Latino," I said matter-of-factly. "A lot of people from the north are blond," I bluffed.

"Good for you, man," he said, concentrating on his drink.

"Are you Latin?" I continued.

"No, I'm from Ohio," he said. Of course, I thought, mocking his non-Latino heritage.

"Anyway, if you ever want to grab a bite, I know this great Spanish restaurant on Forty-ninth Street that I chill at all the time," I said nervously.

I wasn't sure if it was a nod in acknowledgement or him shaking the mixer, but I took it as a "yes."

It worked. I had snared the man I'd obsessed about for the longest time with one simple phrase: "I'm Latin." Who knew that was all it took? I spent the rest of class thinking about my future date with Brett. We'd sip margaritas and nibble on tapas while planning our summer trip to Spain together, and later we'd go back to his place so I could show him a little Latin heat. I got so caught up in my fantasy date that I didn't even notice the rest of the class leaving.

Brett and I were the only two people left except for Harry, who was finishing his spareribs at his desk. It was my golden opportunity to make Brett commit.

"So listen, I wanted to ask you—"

Then, *he* walked in. He was six feet, 180 pounds of beautiful muscle, amazing skin, and a smile that would knock you out cold. The closer I looked at him, the more I realized that he *was* Brett, only Latin.

"What were you saying?" Brett asked.

"It's not important. Just a silly bartending question. I'll see you at class next week," I said meekly.

Brett ignored me and hugged his authentic Latin lothario hello. "I won't be here next week. We have tickets to *Rent*," he said as he walked out of the classroom.

I never returned to bartending class again, dashing a potentially illustrious career as one of New York's top bartenders. I just couldn't bring myself to face the embarrassment and shame I felt.

My mother called me back the next day. "Fifty-five years old and you'd think he could match a shirt with a pair of pants," she lamented. "Did you know I have to color-code his clothes because he wouldn't have a clue what to do? He doesn't get that not everything is meant to go together."

"Uh-huh."

"So, why all the questions about our roots?" she asked.

"It's not important. Let's just say that Dad isn't the only one who didn't know that not everything is meant to go together."

"But I thought the stereotype was that you guys know fashion," she said, not realizing what I truly meant. I never told her any different.

"Not all of us," I joked.

Here I was living in New York City, supposedly "out" and

declaring my gay pride to my family and friends, but after this experience with Brett, I learned it was never a question of being proud to be gay; it was more a question of whether or not I was proud of being me.

Mama Says

In a small town, everyone knows everything about everyone. It wasn't a matter of being a busybody; it was just pretty much the norm for living in a town that had fewer people than half a New York City block. My parents owned the town feed store and a gas station, among other things, so one way or another most people knew who we were. I'm not being boastful or snooty; it's just that everybody needed gas, and almost everyone needed feed in a town primarily of farmers. It didn't bother me, because I didn't know any different.

The summer I turned fourteen, I met my husband. I realize by today's standards that sentence makes it sound like I grew up in some backwoods. Let me *clarify*: I met him at fourteen, although marriage would come a few years later. I knew who he was because he was interested in my friend Linda at the time, but that was about it. A lot of my friends had boyfriends, but not me. I was happy doing my own thing. I've always done my own thing. I was involved in everything at school, from school plays to cheerleading to the band. I couldn't have cared less if I met a boy or not. I was only fourteen.

A few weeks later, my friend clued me in that Ron was interested in *me* and not my friend after all. (Years later, I found out from Ron himself that Linda was just a front to get to me, or so he says. I still think he's full of shit.) I was a lifeguard that summer and he came to the lake and strutted around thinking he was king. I wanted nothing to do with him. Midway through the day, he marched over to me and challenged me to a race. I've never been one to back down from any sort of a challenge, especially from some cocky guy.

The bet was simple—whoever made it to the raft in the middle of the lake first won. I'd swum in that lake probably a hundred times already that month. I wasn't the slightest bit worried. I stood on the edge of the water on one end and Ron stood directly across from me on the other. No sooner did my friend Linda yell "go" than I was diving into the water. I took one giant breath and swam for what seemed like days underwater before returning for a breath of air and then back down into the water. What I didn't know was that when I dove into the water, Ron had run around to the short end of the lake and swum to the raft. After giving all I had, I finally reached the raft to find Ron lying on top of it, asking what took me so long. I knew instantly that he'd cheated. He then had the nerve to expect me to sit on the raft with him. I glared at him, took a deep breath, and swam back to the shore. I wasn't interested in a guy who was arrogant and a cheat. It wasn't the reaction Ron was hoping for, but honestly I didn't care.

I'd pretty much forgotten about the whole thing, including his crush, until the day I went into his dad's grocery store. My mother sent me to pick up a few things for dinner, and I walked in without anyone noticing me. It wasn't until I was picking up some bread that I got a glimpse of Ron. I don't mean physically, I mean spiritually. He was bagging groceries, of all things. I watched the care he took and how kind he was to the older ladies he helped. A neighbor was in the store with her kids, and I watched him try to make her kids laugh by placing grocery bags on his head. As big of a goofball as he was, he was suddenly beautiful to me. I finally saw the real him. It was all over for me from there.

One thing I learned is that you can't ever fix anyone else, whether that person is attracted to you or not. I paid no mind to the Latin heritage thing. Of course, secretly I hoped that at some point Robert would decide to work on shifting his perceptions about who he was as a person, not merely who he was in relation to the gay community. Like everything else in life, when you're not being true to yourself, you generally set yourself up for a drama-filled and unhappy life.

In my own way, I tried to explain to him that he needed to look at who he was becoming as a man. It's nothing new—no one truly knows the shape of the person they'll become. From the little I know from Robert about being gay, it's only one aspect of who a person is. Unfortunately, sometimes people make it the sole component of who they *choose* to be. It's nothing to be ashamed of; rather, it is something to be proud of. And above all else, it's part of completing the wonderful puzzle that you are.

CHAPTER FIFTEEN

Rock Bottom

The lowest point, surprisingly achieved by thousands of gay men every day who have heeded a friend's advice to "open your mind to new experiences," more commonly known as Internet dating

When I first moved to New York in 1996, chatting with strangers on the Internet was something reserved for agoraphobics or sex freaks (although I actually think the two could make a pretty interesting couple). After hearing me bitch and moan about not meeting any men, to the point where my mother told me I was beginning to sound like one of the fag hags I always complained about, my friend Bryan suggested I explore other avenues to meeting a guy.

I resisted at first, but I was told that I needed to open my mind to new experiences if I ever wanted to meet someone. This wasn't what I had in my mind, but I was bored, lonely, and, more importantly, horny. If this wasn't rock bottom, I didn't know what was. Here I was, a promising young theater publicist and almost a bartender. I was young and fairly cute, so why did I have to resort to such tactics? Did I honestly think I'd meet someone special in a chat room? My odds couldn't be very good, considering most normal people were out on dates or with friends on a Friday night. I guess this wasn't what I had envisioned my life to be when I decided to move to New York City and got a job in PR. I thought I'd be having dinner with celebrities that I'd met at launch parties. Boy, was I wrong. Instead of sharing sushi with Renée Zellweger, the pathetic fact of the matter was that there I was, sitting alone in my studio apartment, listening to Sarah McLachlan and writing press releases for work the next day. I was a social midget. Perhaps I could have gone to an event and talked someone's ear off about my client's latest project or world events, but when it came to talking about myself, I broke out into hives.

I finally understood why some of those so-called cyber-geeks never left the safety and security of their computer chat rooms. Could you blame them, especially knowing how cut-throat the New York gay dating scene is? The chat room was a place where all the morons, geeks, and social rejects congregated, and I was praying they'd let me join them. I could feel the "L" on my forehead growing.

Since no one can see each other in a chat room, an insecure, goofy, clumsy guy like me could be a confident, suave, insightful man. All it took was a sharp wit and fast typing skills. I considered myself to have both. Chat rooms weren't a particularly revolutionary idea. In fact, they reminded me of the old party phone lines that I used to see on TV growing up. I remembered seeing the ads on TV, with all these really gorgeous people on the phone talking to each other and thinking it was the coolest thing ever invented. I also loved how the ads made it seem as if these people were talking about religion or the economy when you knew that it was just another means for people to get laid, which was the reason why my mother never let me reach out and "touch" someone. Ten years later, computer chat rooms worked on the same principle. Until now, I was too scared to go onto one out of fear that someone would find out that I was truly a loser.

After about twenty minutes of trying to get into one of the NYC chat rooms, finally I broke through to NYC M4M. It was official: I was the biggest loser in all of New York.

> **RAVE74:** Hi, guys. What's up?

"What's up?" I wrote press releases and bios every day, and that's all I could come up with. I was so lame. It seemed as though my social awkwardness carried over into the written word as well. I was doomed. After two minutes of being ignored, I decided to try again, this time adding a little something extra.

> **RAVE74:** Hi guys. What's up? 22-year-old guy here looking for another cool guy to hang out with.

Two guys—Chris212 and Hotboi2go—responded immediately. I was curious as to who would have the smoothest pickup line. I quickly opened their messages, thinking they were interested.

> **HOTBOI2GO:** No profile. No chat.
> **CHRIS212:** No pic. No meat.

I couldn't believe that I was being dismissed by two total strangers. Not even so much as a hi, hello, or kiss my ass? I soon figured out that in the comforts of your own home, everyone was pretty much straight to the point, abandoning all social graces.

I left the NYC M4M room, went to the profile section of my account, and began filling out the mini-questionnaire. The questions seemed pretty basic.

> **LOCATION:** Manhattan

I wondered if they wanted my street address, but then what if some stalker came to my apartment building and tried to kill me? I had watched several reruns of *Unsolved Mysteries* on Lifetime and had seen it time and time again. I decided to include only my neighborhood so as not to reveal too much.

> **LOCATION:** Manhattan/West Village

The next question was "Sex." *What a redundant question*, I thought. It was the reason I was on the Internet in the first place.

SEX: Yes, thank you.

"Hobbies" was next. I never had time for hobbies, really. I worked, occasionally went out, and then it was home. I did go to the gym; that could work. Oh, and I ate a lot. Could eating be considered a hobby? I typed "working out" and then threw another one in there so I didn't sound so shallow.

HOBBIES: Working out, eating, feeding children in Third World countries

"Marital Status." Nonapplicable, as I wasn't a resident of Vermont.

MARITAL STATUS: Maybe one day with a little luck

"Computers." Hello? Obviously, I had one. How else would I be talking to you people? Who really cared about this category?

COMPUTERS: If you want to know about my computer, we're probably not compatible

"Occupation." That was a little tricky. My job as theater publicist wasn't necessarily going to persuade any manly men to drop their conversation with Tony the construction worker from Brooklyn to talk to a guy who worked with Liza and Julie Andrews. "Bartending school flunkee" didn't have much of a ring to it, either.

OCCUPATION: Yes I have one and it involves people.

"Personal Quote." What? I didn't realize that nowadays you had to be inspirational or witty to get laid. Damn. This was much tougher than I had thought. Screw the personal quote. I was just going to be honest.

> **PERSONAL QUOTE:** Look I'm just a nice guy looking to meet someone that I can share a few laughs with. Oh and get laid too.

I had such a way with words. It was no wonder I was single.

After finishing my profile, I was ready to roll. Even though my first experience wasn't exactly what I had expected, I wasn't ready to abandon all hope just yet. This time I decided to use my PR skills to get some positive results. If there was one thing I had learned about PR, it was that if you weren't aggressive, you might as well not even bother.

I scrolled down the list of names of everyone in the room to see who else was on the prowl. I was shocked at how creative some of these people could be with screen names. At a quick glance, one name jumped out at me. His name was "HotelRoleplay." *Interesting*, I thought. It sounded like he was in from out of town and enjoyed going to the theater. Since I was working in theater PR, I might have an in with him—and hopefully he wouldn't be the typical theater type.

> **RAVE74:** Hey! How's it going?
> **HOTELROLEPLAY:** Good. Cruising.
> **RAVE74:** Where are you from? What kind of work do you do?
> **HOTELROLEPLAY:** I'm looking for some hot role-play.

I hadn't role-played since my high school drama class, and to be quite honest I hated it. I tried to keep an open mind, though.

Maybe I just hadn't found the right role for me yet? Perhaps this guy had a role that was more suitable.

> **RAVE74:** What part would I play?
>
> **HOTELROLEPLAY:** You'd be a janitor at my office building. I'd be working late in my office when you knocked on the door to empty my trash. You'd bend over to pick it up and have a nice surprise waiting for you.

Whoa. This was definitely not the kind of role-play I'd anticipated. I thought now was a good time to see who else was chatting. Before I even looked at the list, an instant message popped up on the screen.

> **AMERICANBUDDY112:** Hey dude. What's up? Nice profile.
>
> **RAVE74:** Thanks. Not much. Just looking to talk with a cool guy.
>
> **AMERICANBUDDY112:** You got one right here. Check my profile and hit me back if you're interested.
>
> **RAVE74:** Ok. Be right back.

It seemed things were getting better. This guy sounded fairly normal and masculine, at least from the screen name and our brief conversation. (The words "dude" and "buddy" implied masculinity to me.) Even if he wasn't, at least he was making the effort. Although considering the last guy, I inspected his profile to make sure.

> **MEMBER NAME:** Christopher
>
> **LOCATION:** NYC-Manhattan Downtown
>
> **SEX:** Male
>
> **MARITAL STATUS:** Single

HOBBIES:

ME: 26 biwm 5'11 170lbs brown/blue very good looking, masculine, nice body but not perfect, mostly smooth, in shape, discreet, healthy (disease/drug free non smoker), nice, fun, and sane!

COMPUTERS:

YOU: Healthy, nonsmoker, masculine, good shape, discreet, funny, and nice

OCCUPATION: $$$

PERSONAL QUOTE: Can you handle me?

Jackpot! This guy sounded amazing. He was around the same age as me, my height, my weight, and masculine. (It was rare to find masculine gay guys these days.) I guessed he wasn't really gay, since his profile said he was bi, but all that really meant was he was too scared to tell his guy friends he wanted to sleep with them. Been there, done that. I also liked that he wasn't some crack addict, like so many gay guys. Drugs were the dowry of gay men for the new millennium. After looking at the rest of his profile, I seemed to match his qualifications. Not that I was shallow, but it looked like he made good money from the dollar signs in the occupation slot. I even imagined bringing a doctor home to meet my parents, or maybe an investment banker. I could live with that.

> **RAVE74:** I think I can handle you just fine. LOL! Great profile.
> **AMERICANBUDDY112:** So what are you into?

Damn! That seemed to be the question of the night on this thing.

> **RAVE74:** Well I'm assuming you don't mean long walks on the beach and the Sunday New York Times. Ha ha. Pretty much anything that's safe. Nothing kinky or weird. I'm just

looking to have a little harmless fun and call it a night. What about you?

AMERICANBUDDY112: I'm extremely aggressive and verbal. Total top here but will switch for the right guy. Oh and I like to cuddle afterwards.

RAVE74: And you're bi? Sounds like you're itching to be a big bottom boy to me.

AMERICANBUDDY112: Huh? I'm totally bi bro.

RAVE74: Ooops! I didn't realize I typed that. Must have been thinking out loud again with my keyboard.

My humor was clearly wasted on this one.

AMERICANBUDDY112: So are you into or not?

RAVE74: Yeah, sure. Why not? Where should we meet?

That had to be some sort of a record. Not even four minutes online and I was going to get laid. No wonder so many gay men I knew were addicted to their computers. Frankly, I was surprised anyone left the house if it was this easy.

AMERICANBUDDY112: I'm looking for company. Go to 60 Horatio Street Buzzer 3C.

RAVE74: Got it. Do you need me to bring anything? Beer? Wine? Chips?

I didn't want to be rude. My mother always taught me to bring something when you're going to someone's house for the first time. I thought the same rule should apply for casual sex, no?

AMERICANBUDDY112: No, I've got everything here lube, rubbers and poppers. Are you paying by cash or credit card?

RAVE74: FOR?

AMERICANBUDDY112: My rate is $350 per hour and $150 every half hour after that.

RAVE74: You're a hooker?

AMERICANBUDDY112: I'm an escort.

RAVE74: I might be desperate, but not that desperate.

AMERICANBUDDY112: What the fuck did you think the $$$ in my profile were?

RAVE74: I thought you were a doctor or something. Sorry I'm not interested. Gotta go. Bye.

I quickly shut off the computer so no one would be able to track my proclivities. All I needed was for someone to find out that I was talking to an escort online. I turned out the lights and hopped into bed, hoping to get some sleep.

That lasted all of three minutes. I pulled the covers back, got out of bed, and sat back down at my computer and signed in again. I suppose I was thinking that if I kept talking to other people about their lives, I wouldn't have to think about my own. This time it was even easier to get into the chat room. It was eleven thirty on a Friday night and this place was like a ghost town. Even the geeks had left.

I felt more comfortable this time, having already been in the chat room, so I went to the kitchen and grabbed a beer. I figured I might as well have a drink to wallow in my self-pity. By the time I returned, there were two instant messages already on my screen. Oh, God. I prayed that it would be someone normal this time. More importantly, please let it be someone who wasn't charging by the hour.

I opened the first one and finally I saw a profile that sounded like everything I had ever been looking for in a man. Six foot one, 185, dark hair and eyes, twenty-eight years old, good job. I immediately began fantasizing about our new life together, me and HOTMASC-JOCK. We'd be together forever.

> **RAVE74:** Hi. Great profile. How are you?
> **HOTMASCJOCK:** Great. You sound hot too. So you looking to hook up?
> **RAVE74:** The thought had crossed my mind, yeah.
> **HOTMASCJOCK:** You have a pic of yourself? Let's do this.

He sent me his before I could even respond to his message to tell him that I, in fact, did not have one. He was breathtaking.

I was typing my response, "Come over now," when another message popped up on my screen from him.

> **HOTMASCJOCK:** I'd love to meet you for a little fun, but I'm too tired to leave my house. Maybe we could have a little fun on here.
> **RAVE74:** What do you mean?
> **HOTMASCJOCK:** I mean what are you wearing right now.

Was this what it had come to, cybersex? Fuck it. If it meant hooking up with this gorgeous guy in the picture, hell yes! I was almost 99 percent sure he wasn't the guy in the picture, but I was willing to go with the fantasy at that hour.

> **RAVE74:** I'm just wearing a pair of sweatpants and no shirt. What about you?

God, I'd seen one too many pornos. If he only knew I was wearing a pair of Joe Boxer pajamas that made me look like I was twelve.

> **HOTMASCJOCK:** Sounds hot bro. I bet you have an awesome body.
>
> **HOTMASCJOCK:** I'm wearing just a pair of boxer briefs and my body looks ripped from the gym.
>
> **HOTMASCJOCK:** Are you still there?
>
> **RAVE74:** I'm here. I was just imagining that gorgeous body of yours. You sound incredible.
>
> **HOTMASCJOCK:** I just took off my boxer briefs.

I couldn't believe I was about to do this. The sad thing was that I was actually turned on by all of it. I had to stop, I told myself. Then I heard the little cartoon devil on my left shoulder whisper in my ear, "What the hell are you doing? You're finally about to get off with a gorgeous guy who's just waiting for you to say the word, and you're having second thoughts! Get over it and do it already!" Clearly, he was smothering the angel on the other shoulder, because no dissenting argument was heard.

> **RAVE74:** I just pulled my sweatpants down. Are you ready for me?
>
> **HOTMASCJOCK:** Oh I'm ready for you bro. I'm just thinking about lying there naked with you. What would you do if I were there right now?
>
> **RAVE74:** I'd begin kissing your lips softly, teasing you with my tongue. Then I'd start licking . . .
>
> **SUPERJ257:** Hey honey! You're up late. What are you doing? You're on my buddy list now! I'm just logging my points on the new weight watchers website. Isn't that neat?
>
> **RAVE74:** Hi Mother . . .

Mama Says

Internet dating.

I don't like it. It scares me and I am not ashamed to say it. I know it's a generational thing, but let's be honest, there are so many weir-does out there. They say there's somewhere around 210 million people who have surfed the Internet at one time or another. Not to sound like an old lady, but the closest thing we had to Internet dat-ing when I was young was going out on a blind date. You would have thought people would have learned something from the nightmares of blind dates, but instead some socially inept moron created Internet chat rooms to enable chatters to set up mini-dates every three or four minutes. Some say it's a breakthrough in the search for love. I say it's a way to stay home and waste your life away in front of a computer screen.

Gay or straight, we live in a world where people turn their noses up at others every day because they are not a model for Victoria's Secret or Abercrombie & Fitch. I hate to break it to everyone, but these people long for love, too. God forbid anyone actually put themselves out there and speak to someone in today's world. No one wants to be vulnerable, so we sit in the comfort of our homes and type into a machine so we don't face rejection. A simple, "Hi, how are you?" doesn't translate to "Let's get married!" It simply means, "Hi, how are you?" Ask directions. Give directions. Ask about a good place to eat. I always heard growing up that one must be a friend before one can find a friend. There are a great many people in this world that have hearts of gold. Give them a chance. Try being nice to someone. He or she just might surprise you, and you will find a best friend, or possibly more.

On the other hand, they could also be a complete nut job.

CHAPTER SIXTEEN
The Daughter-in-Law You'll Never Have

Also known to my parents as my best friend Melissa

I met my best friend Melissa in a business French class in college and surprisingly we were both wearing chocolate brown velvet pants. Even more surprising was the fact that neither one of us acknowledged my obvious gayness. I was too closeted to mention it and she was too mesmerized by a boy in velvet to care. When I rather emphatically told Melissa these pants were, in fact, made for men, she sort of shot me a look that said *Keep telling yourself that, sister.* However, as the professor was about to stress the importance of the global community to the class, Melissa leaned in and said, "We're going to be best friends from this moment on."

After undergoing yet another dating disaster, I called to vent to Melissa. I told her I was going to be one of those old, bitter, snarky, gay men that you see sipping martinis in piano bars listening to showtunes.

"You hate musicals," Melissa said.

"You're missing my point." I heard some commotion in the background. "Are you at work?"

"Yeah, it's fine. Juvenile felony. He's most likely going to go to juvy," she said. Melissa is a public defender for the city of Chicago. She'd been offered several other high-paying jobs at private law firms, but she instead chose to work as a public defender.

"Can he hear you?" I asked.

"Probably," she said.

"Oh, so anyway . . . I'd love to see you one of these days. It's been way too long and I could really use some time with you."

"I'll book it after work. How's the weekend after next?" she asked.

"Wow. Yeah, sure, that would be incredible." I wasn't expecting her to come so soon, but that was typical of Melissa. She'd be there as soon as she could. This meant a great deal to me, especially knowing her grueling work schedule. I was blessed to have such a friend like Melissa. I could truly be myself around her.

"We're not only going to gay bars this time, right?" she asked.

Or not.

"Um, no, we don't have to. I hadn't even thought about what we would do yet."

"I just want the possibility of meeting an actual straight man this time," she said. "And don't get all gay pride parade on me. I'm only saying that we need to go to places where there's a chance for both of us to meet a guy."

I suddenly realized that this trip was going to be mutually beneficial. Melissa would cheer me up, and she would in turn meet a straight man. One of Melissa's dreams is to marry the real-life Tony Soprano. No, seriously. If he was short, with a protruding, ravioli-filled belly, and wore lots of gold, he would be next to heaven for her. Therefore, whenever there was an opportunity to meet a real mobster to fall in love with and marry, she was on the next American Airlines flight. My dad often asked how her search for the mobster was going. I quickly reminded them both that she worked for the city of Chicago and that her job would scare off any potential organized crime prospects. Melissa retaliated by telling us both that she was a public *defender*, not a *prosecutor*. Semantics, I argued.

"Okay, we can do that."

"Listen, I got to run. This kid is still not telling me the truth and he doesn't know what can happen in juvy."

"Like *you* know? I'm sure you're about to tell him something you saw in some bad movie," I said.

"A hundred percent," she said.

A few weeks later, Melissa arrived at my tiny studio apartment around eight in the evening. She was tired from having to work all day, so we decided it would be best to stay in, order food, and open a bottle of wine or two.

After two glasses, Melissa very seriously informed me, "This night counts as our gay night."

"Wow. All right. Look, I told you already that with my present luck with guys I'm completely okay with that," I said.

"That's what you say now. I know we're going to be out tomorrow and you're going to want to go gaying."

"I won't. You're my priority tomorrow," I said.

"That makes me nervous. The last time that you made me your priority you told me I was too old to have J-Lo hair and that now I look like Calista Flockhart during the *Ally McBeal* years."

"Look, you *are* too old for J-Lo hair. You're not sixteen and going to the mall on Saturday afternoons. Besides, nobody wants an attorney who has hair down to her back."

"You called me Melissa 'No-pez.'"

"Meh. I like to think of it as an intervention." We opened another bottle of wine like any self-respecting best friends from college would do. "Now for the love of God, can we please talk about me? Hello? You came out here to cheer *me* up," I said, and filled Melissa's glass.

She got up from the couch and announced, "I'm going to your balcony to smoke."

"Or not."

When Melissa and I are together it's like sticking two people with attention deficit disorder in the same room and asking them to read *Ulysses*. A million different and completely random topics will be spit out rapid-fire. We've never tried to be polite friends with each other; we simply tell one another exactly how we feel, no matter what. Fortunately, we're usually thinking the same thing. When this happens, we tell each other to scratch the imaginary scar on our faces that obviously separated us at birth as if we had been Siamese twins sharing the same brain.

I followed Melissa out to my tiny balcony on the twenty-fifth floor and stared down Amsterdam Avenue. She turned to me and said, "I'm so proud of you. You know that, right?"

"Proud? I'm twenty-four and an assistant at a PR firm. I think proud is a stretch." I laughed.

"No, you went after what you wanted. Most people don't have the guts to do it," she said, and took a drag of her cigarette.

"You're a lawyer in Chicago. It's not like you're twiddling your thumbs in Podunk."

"I know, but what I'm trying to tell you is that you need to stop focusing on what's not happening in your life and start focusing on what *is* good in it. Otherwise, fuck off," she said. She took another sip of her drink and turned to face the Hudson River.

"You have such a way with words," I said and laughed. "A real wordsmith."

"Shut up. You know what I mean."

"I do and I appreciate it," I said. We shared a quiet moment and took in the Manhattan skyline. She was right. I was living my dream. The sounds of the cars honking below me, the twinkling lights in the brisk night air, everything. This was what I had always wanted and here it was surrounding me. We were still for a few more minutes until finally I broke the silence and said, "So this guy I went on a date with . . ."

"Oh Jesus, I'm going to bed."

I laughed at Melissa as she turned to face the door. I knew it would elicit a reaction from her. "Okay, okay. I get it."

"Let's have a really fun day tomorrow, please?" she said. "Okay, buddy?"

"As opposed to a really shitty day?" I laughed. "Yes, you got it." She put out her cigarette, had one last sip of wine, and went inside and crashed on my pullout sofa.

I woke up the next morning around eleven and Melissa was already in the shower ready to start the day. I thought it was a good idea to go to the fridge and take out one of two remaining pieces of old birthday cake. I couldn't quite remember whose birthday party it was from or how old this particular piece was, but it was unimportant at that moment. I also grabbed a Diet Coke to wash down my ultra-healthy breakfast. I knew I was going to need as much energy as possible to keep up with Melissa. If my meal gave me a temporary sugar high, then so be it, as long as it worked. I knew I could always recharge in a bakery later.

I took my breakfast to the couch and turned on the television. I flipped through several channels before stopping on *My Best Friend's Wedding*. I wasn't exactly sure what time Melissa went into my bathroom to begin her transformation into a human being again, but I was certain I had plenty of time to spend with Julia Roberts before I had to go. I turned the movie on at the scene where Julia asks her gay best friend, played by Rupert Everett, to pretend that they are engaged and madly in love. This was all to make Julia's best friend, Michael, jealous in order to win his heart away from his fiancée. Their scheme started out great and was actually quite believable. However, the chinks in their armor began to show. I couldn't handle the stress of Julia being caught in a lie. I returned to the kitchen and grabbed the last piece of cake and another Diet Coke. I plopped back down on the couch and saw that disaster had struck for poor Julia. That's right: It's all fun and games until a table full of middle-aged men and women sing Dionne Warwick at brunch. However, due to the sugar and the caffeine, I joined them in song. I had hoped my bad singing would prompt some sort of sign of life from my bathroom, but nothing came.

Nearly an hour and a half later, Melissa emerged, looking like she'd just left a photo shoot for *Elle* magazine. Anything was possible since she'd been getting ready for so long. She was finally ready to head out. I, on the other hand, was in a sugar coma.

"Come on, let's go," Melissa said.

"I can't move. I think it's the cake," I said and groaned.

"Grab a Diet Coke out of the fridge to settle your stomach and we'll stop at a Starbucks somewhere to get you back in the game," she said. Diet Coke, I'd decided, was like water for Midwesterners, or anyone for that matter who didn't live in New York or Los Angeles. Diet Coke was the cure-all. Have a headache? Have some Diet Coke. Hungover? A large Diet Coke with ice. Tired? Go for the two-liter bottle of Diet Coke.

I nodded at her and she helped me off the couch. "Where do you want to go first?" I grumbled.

"Shopping."

"Of course," I said as I grabbed my Diet Coke and shut the front door behind me.

Shopping was a sport for Melissa and she could teach those yentas on *What Not to Wear* a thing or two about fashion and more importantly where to find the best deals. However, Melissa's wardrobe mainly consisted of one color: black. Everything in her closet was just different shirts, pants, skirts, and dresses in black. So why she needed to continue to shop for more variations of the same exact thing was beyond me. But I knew not to argue; she was a lawyer and that would exhaust me.

The first couple of stores we went to we were in and out of without so much as a single bag. I looked at my watch and it was already three thirty. Melissa knew that I was thinking of afternoon cocktails.

"Listen, boozy Suzy, we're not going to happy hour just yet. I need to find some cute clothes," she said, flipping through a rack of black belts.

"God, you're good. It's seriously scary sometimes how much you know me," I said.

"It's a gift. Well, that and you're predictable," she said.

Suddenly a salesperson popped out from behind one of the racks, looked at Melissa and said, "My boyfriend hates shopping with me, too." Melissa stood holding onto a patent leather belt in stunned silence. The saleswoman turned her attention toward me. "You're such a good boyfriend. I'm sure you'll get a special treat at the end of the day for being such a good sport," she said and winked.

I looked at Melissa, who was ignoring the salesclerk. "Does she mean like a cookie?" I asked. "'Cause I could go for a chocolate chip cookie."

Melissa smirked and was unable to speak. It didn't matter because the saleswoman was more than happy to continue speaking for the both of us.

"If you're anything like my boyfriend, I'm sure you're hating every minute of this," the stranger said with a plastic smile on her face.

"Oh, you don't even know how much I'm hating this right now," I said and mirrored her fake smile back at her.

"Let me know if I can help you with anything else," the saleslady said before disappearing back into the racks from which she came.

"Can you believe the nerve?" Melissa said with a grimace.

"I know! She mentioned her boyfriend in almost every sentence," I said. "Well, screw you, lady, not all of us have boyfriends." I began to laugh. I wasn't sure if the salesgirl was still within earshot. We decided we better make a mad dash for the exit before the boyfriend-crazed saleswoman returned.

We left the store and walked the streets of SoHo, deep in conversation. Yet I kept noticing that we were the lucky recipients of a plethora of warm smiles and nods from couples as they passed by. Somewhere between Varick and Grand, Melissa and I had unconsciously locked arms as we often did when walking together.

"Are you noticing this, too?" I asked. "You realize people think we're a couple, don't you?"

"Yeah, it's kinda creepy—like secret-society creepy," Melissa said. "But I have to say you're the perfect 'man-cessory.'"

"I'm not sure if I should thank you or tell you to fuck off since you just equated me to one of your purses or watches," I said as we hailed a taxi to go to Central Park and sit in Sheep Meadow.

"Take it how you want it," she said.

"Is that what you tell guys when you meet them?" I said and laughed.

"Why do I even bother with you?"

"Because you love me," I said as I sat down in the back of the taxi.

"I do love you," Melissa said and squeezed my shoulder.

Our cab driver looked at us in the rearview mirror as we headed uptown and asked in a thick accent, "You two married?"

"Well, I've been trying to make an honest woman of her for the last five years, but she's not having any of it," I said.

Melissa turned and looked at me. "Since when did you become Southern? An honest woman? Not having any of it? You're kidding, right?"

I nudged her arm in an effort to go along with my hoax. I mean, seriously, how else were we going to kill time in traffic?

"That's only because he can't settle down with only me. He wants to have his cake *and* eat it, too," Melissa said. The cabbie laughed and I noticed he was giving me the equivalent of an eye high-five through the mirror.

"You can't blame me, right, sir?" I said, verbalizing our brotherhood.

"He has a point, ma'am. We are men," the cab driver explained.

"Yeah, we're men," I said, feeling a bit cocky in my new male solidarity.

"Men have needs," he said.

"Do those needs include sleeping with other men, sir?" Melissa said.

"What?" the cabbie said, not sure if he understood Melissa correctly.

"Do your needs include sleeping with other men?" she repeated.

I elbowed Melissa. Hard. "Are you crazy? I don't want him to issue a fatwa on my ass."

Melissa ignored my pleas for mercy. "I'm simply saying that if he can sleep with another man on the weekends, so can I. It's only fair. What do you think, sir?"

"I'm going to kill you," I whispered to Melissa.

"Not if he kills you first," Melissa replied.

She was right. I studied our driver's cab number and name thinking these would be the last things I saw before I was murdered somewhere in Midtown. "What do you think?" Melissa asked him again.

"I think I'm done talking," he said.

After a sufficiently awkward fifteen-minute cab ride, we finally got out at Sixty-seventh Street and walked to one of my favorite spots in Manhattan, Sheep Meadow in Central Park. Everyone from all walks of life converges on this huge and meticulously kept grassy lawn. Melissa staked out a space next to some shirtless Frisbee players.

"I thought you might like it here," Melissa said and sat down. I joined her in the grass. Here we were, in one of the most beautiful parks in the world, surrounded by some of the most incredibly designed buildings, watching three shirtless guys playing Frisbee.

"I'm so glad you came," I said without taking my eyes off the boy in the gray shorts.

"Me, too," Melissa said. "I like the one in the navy shorts."

"He's all yours. I like the one in the gray."

"Aww, now I feel bad for the not as attractive one in the black shorts," Melissa said.

"Really, Melissa? You would even mercy fuck someone in your fantasy? What is wrong with you?" I said and smiled.

"I'm a sucker for the underdog," she said.

"Yes, you are."

Melissa's smile faded and she looked at me very seriously and then said, "I feel like I missed my opportunity to be friend of the year," she said.

"What? Why?"

"Here you were sharing this huge part of your life when you came out to me and I was surrounded by a ton of people and couldn't say a word to anyone yet. I felt like I failed as a friend," Melissa said.

"You most certainly didn't fail. You excelled. You've been the most incredible friend to me, and I don't know where I would be without your friendship. You are like family to me. It's like the mob; now that you're in, *you're in*," I said.

"Speaking of the mob, can we please go find me a mobster boyfriend? I've waited long enough," Melissa said, standing up.

"What about these guys playing Frisbee?"

"They're so gay and you've known that since we sat down," Melissa said.

"Yeah, you're right, I did," I said, standing up. "Okay, let's go find you Tony Soprano Jr." Melissa's eyes lit up and we walked across the park into Midtown West. "Do you want to run home and shower and then we can head downtown to one of the straight clubs?"

"No, let's stay in Midtown. This is where my husband is going to be, I can feel it. He's not going to be at some hipster hangout."

"But the places in Midtown are tourist traps," I said.

"I don't care. We're going," she said, point-blank.

There was only one place I remembered off the top of my head that was in Midtown, and against my better judgment, I promised that we would go there. After eating dinner and having several drinks at The Saloon across from Lincoln Center, we walked over to the bar. I was committed to making her America's Next Guidette even if it literally killed me.

After standing in line to get into some hideous nightclub, we had to stand in another line to pay a cover charge.

"You realize that I'd rather drink an entire bottle of Maalox than go into this bar, right?"

"You said tonight was going to be my night," Melissa insisted.

"I did. I don't know why I picked such a tourist bar. We might as well have gone to Planet Hollywood or a hotel bar next to the JFK airport. It's really going to be the same type of people," I argued.

I realized this sounded incredibly rude, but Melissa wasn't getting it. I guess she was going to have to see it for herself to believe me. We made our way to the cashier and the cover was twenty-five dollars. I handed the guy fifty bucks and we went inside. I might be gay, but there is something incredibly old-fashioned in me that doesn't like it if I'm with a woman and she pays. It's not meant to be chauvinistic in the slightest. I learned it from watching my dad and older brother and it sort of stuck with me.

"I'm giving you money for that. I'm a lawyer. I can pay for myself."

"Easy, Judge Judy, you're a public defender. I'll pick this one up." She hit me in the arm as she often does when I say something inappropriate or rude. We managed to walk three steps before being stopped by a giant metal detector.

"I can really pick 'em," Melissa said before being patted down.

"You sure can," I said as the three-hundred-pound bouncer squeezed the inside of my thigh. "I hope the prostate exam is next," I called out to Melissa.

The bouncer quickly interrupted and mumbled, "Go through."

We walked inside the cavernous club, and by "cavernous" I mean it smelled like a dark, musty cave.

"We wouldn't have had to pay if we went to a gay bar," I said as we made our way deeper inside.

"No, I would still be standing outside waiting and they would've let you go right in," Melissa said.

"It's pretty great, isn't it?" I said.

The music was pumping through the speakers. Thankfully, it was old-school hip-hop, one of my favorites. "This reminds me of the music we used to play at my fraternity parties, don't you think?" Melissa either didn't hear me or was simply ignoring me. We surveyed the room and it was pretty obvious what we would find: Every guy looked like a cheesy tourist stereotype and every girl was dressed like a video ho.

"I swear this usually is much more fun after a few drinks," Melissa said and laughed.

"I feel like I'm getting herpes on my feet," I said as we walked across the slippery dance floor.

We made our way to the bar and ordered our usual vodka and sodas. Melissa paid for the drinks while I watched some woman make sweet love to one of the speakers. We hadn't even downed half of our drinks before a man darted over. I saw this mess coming from across the bar, in part because of his loud shirt, and I thought it would be a waste of a night in Midtown to not let this moment happen. I told Melissa that I needed to use the little boy's room. Under the cover of darkness, I quickly disappeared and ducked behind one of the large gothic columns in the corner of the room. She never knew what hit her.

In his electric orange polo and pleated khakis he danced over to Melissa. He looked like he was on loan from the eighties—and not in a chic retro way. I couldn't hear his pickup line because Rob

Base was playing too loudly over the speakers. Yes, Rob Base. I felt like the chicken dance or the Macarena was going to be coming on the sound system at any moment. I assumed he was slightly drunk or at least I hoped that he was because of the way he was dancing. I moved in for a closer look.

"You and me, the dance floor. Now," the man said and pointed to the orgy of The Gap and Eddie Bauer taking place in the center of the room. *Wait a second. Was he just doing "the robot"? Oh. My. God. This man is an absolute catch. She has to marry him.* I thought about returning to save Melissa, but this was just too good. Besides, if there were a sharp object nearby, I knew Melissa would have jammed it into my eye.

However, the incredible thing about Melissa is that she's up for anything. She'll dance, she'll drink, she'll laugh. She's always game for any adventure that's thrown at her. She followed him out to the dance floor and once she was there she slowly swayed back and forth, while he looked like he was having a seizure.

As Melissa and her new lover were dancing, I rested my back against the bar and enjoyed my momentous victory. Then I felt a tap on my shoulder.

"Excuse me," this young blond woman said to me.

"Hi. Yes?" I said.

"I was wondering if you wouldn't mind dancing with my friend. Her boyfriend just broke up with her, and she really could use the cheering up."

"Wow, that sucks. I'm sorry to hear that. But I have to be honest, I'm a really bad dancer," I said. "Embarrassingly bad," I said to punctuate my point.

"It doesn't matter!" she said excitedly. She gently pushed me in the direction of her friend.

"No, really I am."

"Who cares? Everyone is a bad dancer here," she said. She got me on that one. This was some of the worst dancing I'd seen to date. This was wedding dancing bad.

"Also, there's something else you should know . . ." I said.

"Listen, I think you're losing focus here. Get out on the dance floor!" she said and shoved me toward the whirling dervish known as her best friend.

"I'm gay," I said mid-shove.

"I'm sorry?" she said.

"I'm gay."

"You're a real asshole," she said and furrowed her brow.

"Not quite the reaction I was expecting, yet I'm not completely surprised," I said. I now stood on the dance floor with people doing variations on the electric slide, break dancing, and every other dance that involved arm-flapping.

"I can't believe you said that you're gay so you wouldn't have to dance with my friend. What kind of person does that?"

"A gay one," I responded.

She rolled her eyes, grabbed her friend by the arm, pulled her off the dance floor, and retreated to the ladies' room. Feeling like a complete pariah, I did the walk of shame back to the bar. Thankfully, my spirits were lifted again when I saw Melissa. By that time, her "date" had moved on from doing the "running man" to the more refined "sprinkler" in the middle of the dance floor. Even better was that every time Melissa tried to escape he would grab her hand and pull her back out. She tried making eye contact with me at several points to signal an SOS. Naturally, I looked everywhere but her eyes. She was the one who wanted to come here, so I wanted her to have the full experience.

I turned my back to her and ordered another vodka and soda. I felt something graze my back, but told myself it was probably some girl's purse rubbing against me as she walked by. The bartender handed me my drink and as I was about to take a sip, I felt something hit my head. I turned around and flashed a nasty look at no one in particular and handed the bartender the money for the drink. Then I was pelted right at the base of my neck with a piece of ice. I turned around to find the woman and her friend staring at me with a full cup of ice.

"Asshole," she mouthed.

I cocked my head back. I had seriously never seen this type of aggression. Instead of stooping to her level and mouthing something equally as nasty back, I moved out of her firing range.

By now Melissa's new lover was trying to do the bump and grind. This wasn't going to end well . . . for him. I decided to intercede before having to eventually bail Melissa out of jail for battery. I bobbed and weaved through the throngs of Club MTV castaways and grabbed Melissa's hand.

"What do you think you're doing?" the dancing machine shouted.

Before I could say a word, Melissa shouted at him, "He's my boyfriend!"

I was expecting to have a full-on bar fight in the middle of Midtown. Instead, he shrugged and said, "Your loss." He danced away from us and was soon enveloped by the crowd.

"Wow, Carlton from *The Fresh Prince of Bel-Air* looks great," I said.

"That's weird, I was thinking the same thing. He danced like a white Carlton," she said and nodded.

"Scratch the scar," I said.

And with that, Melissa and I walked off the dance floor, holding hands, with giant smiles on our faces. We were almost out the door to safety when we ran into the horny dance-floor girl.

"Asshole!" Miss Congeniality shouted.

"Hey!" Melissa snapped back. "Do NOT call my boyfriend an asshole!"

"You're a fucking dog!" the woman shouted as we made our way out the door. "Gay? My ass!" she said before the door shut.

"What was that about?" Melissa asked as I hailed a taxi.

"I think I was being straight-bashed. Thank God we can end this awful charade now and I can go back to being a happy-go-lucky, carefree gay guy," I said.

"Yeah, because carefree is exactly how I would describe you," Melissa said as she got into the car.

We slunk into the backseat like it was the most comfortable couch on the planet. We were exhausted. It takes a lot of work to be a straight couple. Melissa and I were silent for most of the cab ride home. We were too tired to speak in complete sentences and felt like our intellect had pretty much been raped. So instead, I did what I thought was the most appropriate thing to do at that time.

"From the moment I wake up . . ." I sang.

Without missing a beat, Melissa responded with, "Before I put on my makeup . . ."

And in unison, we sang, "I say a little prayer for you."

Scratch the scar.

Mama Says

As parents, we all want pretty much the same things for our kids: for them to be happy, successful, and to have a family of their own. Maybe not always in that order, but that is what we hope at least will happen.

Every parent visualizes their first meeting with their child's future spouse. I'm not telling some forbidden secret or anything, it's simply the reality of being a parent. We all have some grand fairy tale in our mind about what exactly our children's future will be. Whether it's cooking Sunday roast in the kitchen with your future daughter-in-law or playing cards with your future son-in-law, there's a fantasy scenario that plays on a loop in a parent's head. Personally, I blame Julia Roberts and Sandra Bullock and every other romantic comedy for this notion. However, we know deep in our heart of hearts that at some point that first introduction will take place. My dream meeting went something like this:

I received the phone call from Robert. He's met "the one." He tells me that I'm going to love her. She's gorgeous, smart, and incredibly down to earth. She comes from a wonderful family on the East Coast. They summer on Martha's Vineyard and they want Ron and me to come out for two weeks every summer. She's a pediatrician, but also wants to have a family. She also does a great deal of philanthropy around the world.

Obviously, when Robert flew home to introduce us to her, it would be something out of a fairy tale. She would bring me a basket of various coffees and biscotti from my favorite gourmet deli, Dean & DeLuca in New York. Robert didn't tell her that these were my favorite. She just knew. We hugged and felt an instant familial connection. She was one of us. She sat in the kitchen and sipped wine with my daughter and me and we joked about Robert's neuroses. She found it cute and endearing. She was kind and treated me with respect. She was polite and refined. She loved my son above all else. At the end of our time together, we would hug, wipe our respective tears away, and would be in touch to plan a bridal shower. Ron and I would drive them to the airport, and blast Sister Sledge's "We Are Family" along the way with all of us singing along with the chorus.

That was how all of this was supposed to occur. . . .

As I have come to realize, things don't always happen the way we imagine. I was hosting a luncheon at my house for some friends and a few family members. I rarely did these kinds of things so I wanted to make sure everything went smoothly. I had asked Robert if there were any of his female friends that wanted to help me out with my ladies-only open house/tea party. He asked around and told me that he found two friends of his that wanted to earn some extra cash.

A few days before my event, I received an e-mail from Robert:

> From: Robert Rave
> To: Jane Rave
> Time: May 3 10:42AM
> Subject: MELISSA
>
> Hey. I'm going to bring my friend Melissa by so she can help out with that tea you're having at the house. She's pretty incredible and I think you're going to really like her. I know she's there to help out and work, but be extra nice, I really like this one.
> R

Robert really liked this one? She's "pretty incredible" and "I'm going to really like her." I couldn't believe what I was reading. This could be his future wife! Robert brought different girls home from time to time for us to meet. They were always very cute, smart, and generally I liked each and every one of them. More importantly, these girls usually seemed to really like my son . . . a lot.

I showed the e-mail to my husband. He didn't share in my excitement.

"Yeah, and?" he said after reading it.

"Do you think this is the one?" I asked.

"I don't think so," he said.

"But why?" I protested. "Robert has talked about her to me several times before. 'Melissa this' and 'Melissa that.' They are always together and Robert often tells me how much she makes him laugh," I added.

"I don't think she's the one. Maybe," Ron said without giving it much thought.

I knew I loved her already. I have been and always will be a hopeless romantic at heart. I quickly sat down at my computer to respond to Robert's e-mail.

From: Jane Rave
To: Robert Rave
Sent: May 3 11:19AM
Subject: RE: MELISSA

Hello,
I'm not sure why you thought I wouldn't be nice to Melissa,
but of course I will be extra nice to her. It sounds like you
really like her a great deal. Why doesn't she come to the tea
and not work it? I'd love to get to know her better.
Mom

I hit send and sat back in my chair and thought well, here comes the happy part for Robert with perhaps a family to come. Hopefully, the family part wouldn't come until much later. I sat in my chair grinning and Ron walked by.

"What are you smiling about?" he asked.

"Our son finding someone to share his life with," I said.

"You need to switch to decaf coffee," Ron said and continued walking.

After a few minutes, I received another e-mail in my inbox.

From: Robert Rave
To: Jane Rave
Sent: May 3, 11:37AM
Subject: RE: RE: MELISSA

No mom, you're missing the point. She wants to work to make extra money. She's looking forward to meeting you too. Please don't be weird. She's there to work not have tea with a bunch of ladies.
R

I immediately hit respond.

From: Jane Rave
To: Robert Rave
Sent: May 3, 11:39AM
Subject: RE: RE: RE: MELISSA

Someone clearly got up on the wrong side of the bed. I was only asking if your "friend" wanted to join the tea instead of working it. Sorry. How am I weird?
Mom

I sat in front of my computer for another thirty minutes waiting for the little shit to respond. Ron walked by again.

"What are you doing?" he asked.

"Waiting for Robert to answer my e-mail," I said.

"What happened?" Ron asked.

"He got all in a tizzy because I said his friend could join the tea instead of work and he said I was being weird," I explained.

"Good luck with that," Ron said and disappeared again.

Finally, my inbox lit up.

From: Robert Rave
To: Jane Rave
Sent: May 3, 12:34PM
Subject: RE: RE: RE: RE: MELISSA

Why did you put "friend" in quotes? What the hell does that mean? She's friend NOT "friend" whatever that means. I'll see you on Friday with my FRIEND Melissa.
-R

Friday arrived before I knew it. I made sure the house looked immaculate. I prepared a great meal and anxiously waited for them to arrive. And by *them* I meant Robert and Melissa. Robert had told me that he would drop Melissa off and pick her up after we were done. My other guests had become an afterthought. I don't know why I was so nervous but I was, maybe my inner self was setting me up for what was to come. Ron had left since it was a girls-only day so I didn't have anyone else there to calm my nerves. I was setting up for the luncheon when I heard Robert coming in through the side door.

"Mom?" he yelled.

Here we go, I thought. "In here," I said from my living room. I heard them walking through the house and I took a deep breath in.

"Hey, Mom," he said.

"Hi," I said and exhaled. I caught a glimpse of Melissa and she was a beautiful brunette with stunning eyes. She gave me a big smile. I hoped this was the one. I liked her already.

"This is Melissa. The one I was telling you about," he said.

"Hi, Melissa. I've heard so much about you from Robert. He goes on and on about you," I said. "He likes you so much!" Robert shot me a confused look.

"Hopefully, he says all good things. You never know what comes out of his mouth."

"Anyway, I have to get back to campus," Robert said, looking at Melissa. "Call me when you want me to pick you up."

Robert hugged me good-bye and left Melissa and me alone. The more we talked, the more I liked everything about her. She was pretty. She had a great personality and made me laugh. I could see why Robert was enamored with her. I listened as she told me what she wanted to do in life and I was very impressed. A defense attorney who helped those less fortunate? Who wouldn't want that for their son? As we finished prepping for the party, she said how much she loved Robert. At the time, I didn't realize she meant platonically. I thought this was the one.

My open house was a big success, but what was more of a success was the friendship that I had formed with someone so special to Robert. I loved Melissa's spunk and sassiness. We kept in touch after that day and occasionally met for breakfast and e-mailed each other every now and then. For all intents and purposes she had become a part of the family.

So when Robert announced that he was moving to New York, I sent him the following e-mail.

From: Jane Rave
To: Robert Rave
Sent: June 8, 1:24PM
Subject: Melissa

Is Melissa upset that you're moving to New York? Do you think she'll move as well? I miss her. You should invite her over.

A few hours went by before I got a response from Robert.

From: Robert Rave
To: Jane Rave
Sent: June 8, 4:47PM
Subject: RE: Melissa

Why would Melissa be mad that I'm moving to New York? She's incredibly excited for me. She's back in Chicago. I'm sure I'll see her once before I leave. I'll see if she wants to get together with all of us my first trip back from New York.
–R

Judging from Robert's e-mail, it sounded as if he and Melissa weren't as serious as I had thought or hoped. When Robert did come out to us approximately four months later, one of the first people I thought of was Melissa. How did she take the news? Was she crushed? Angry? Did she know before us?

All of my questions would be answered over Sunday brunch nearly six months after Robert came out to Ron and me, and during his first visit home. I was so excited to see her again.

"How are you?" I asked.

"I can't believe it's been this long," Melissa said and gave me a big hug.

There were only a few moments of awkwardness and that was only because when we met Melissa before, we thought, or at least I thought, I was meeting Robert's future wife. She hadn't known Robert was gay before we did. She suspected, but Robert waited to tell us before he told her.

To break the ice, Melissa said, "Well, I guess you can think of me as the daughter-in-law that you'll never have." The entire table erupted in laughter.

However, I looked at it very differently. "You may not be our daughter-in-law, but we certainly think of you as one of the family," I said.

Even if Melissa wouldn't be our daughter-in-law I loved her like one. She is a great friend to both Ron and me and to Robert as well. She calls me whenever she is in town for college reunions or on business. We go to lunch, shop together—what more could I ask for? It felt just like the dream I'd always imagined. Sure, there were a few alterations to that dream, but that is perfectly okay with this mother.

CHAPTER SEVENTEEN
Masochism

Inviting your friend who just moved from Miami to crash with you in your studio apartment while he looks for his own place (oh, and your friend is a hot male model)

From as early as I can remember I have been obsessed with the entertainment industry. I was always captivated by the spectacle of it all. I still blame my mother for this. She spent most of her pregnancy either in front of the television watching soap operas or playing too much Carly Simon on the eight-track, and I'm still feeling the horrible repercussions.

Like most kids (or so I thought), I'd put on shows for my family members at every major family event. You name it—Christmas, birthdays, and, yes, even funerals, there I was, anxiously waiting to put on a new show. Unfortunately for my audience, there was a new show approximately every thirty minutes, and I insisted that they sit through every last gut-wrenching minute. In most cases, I'd make it up as I'd go. Shakespeare in the Park it was not.

My brother was baffled that I'd rather do these silly little shows than play basketball outside with him. To him, I was some sort of enigma. I was the kid that negotiated playing Little League football for two summers under the strict condition that my parents subscribe to the Disney channel for an extra five bucks a month. My brother most likely viewed me as a freak of sorts. I didn't mind. Other kids had Dungeons & Dragons. I had Mickey and some fucked-up dog named Goofy. I loved living in a fantasy world even then, and I continued to love it after I moved to New York. It was much easier to live vicariously through the glamourpusses than to face the reality that I was a flat-nosed, no-lipped, overweight, just-off-the-farm kid.

I met my friend Billy at another friend's birthday party in a loft in the West Village. We instantly connected, in part because we were the only two there that were under thirty and also because he was a hot young model (a minor detail).

Billy was gorgeous. Six foot two, blond hair, brown eyes, and a stomach that most men would kill for (or, in a lot of cases, pay for). We both knew immediately that there was no mutual sexual attraction. He wasn't Latin, and Latin, I had discovered, was my latest ethnicity of preference. I, on the other hand, just *wasn't*. Thankfully, we were on safe and even ground, which eliminated all the typical fake bullshit you have to go through when you first meet someone that you might want to date and/or sleep with. The more we drank, the more we hit it off. Soon after, I learned that Billy booked a few modeling jobs in New York, but as of yet he didn't have a place to stay. I was mesmerized with someone who actually worked in entertainment instead of being a mere observer like me at my PR job. I casually offered him the pullout sofa bed in my 550-square-foot apartment. He immediately accepted, proclaiming our new lifelong friendship. "It will only be for a week or so," he swore. I went home alone and woke up with a hangover and hobbled into work the next morning.

The morning flew by, and I had trouble remembering much of what had occurred just six hours prior. I walked to Bryant Park during my lunch hour to clear my muddled head. I loved to people watch. (Some call it spacing out, but I preferred the less abrasive term.) There is nothing better to do when nursing a hangover than watch all the drama that exists in other people's lives. It reassured me that I wasn't as pathetic as I'd often thought. It was ideal lunchtime entertainment, and I was too broke to afford a Wednesday matinee ticket. This was a poor man's Broadway, and I had orchestra seats.

The only problem with nursing a hangover is that you often start re-evaluating your life. I'd have internal fights, telling the right side of my brain to shut up and just enjoy the zoning out. Unfortunately, that side often ended up winning, as it did that day, and I started to reflect on my career in theater PR.

I knew I never quite fit in working in theater PR. I always felt like I was a used car salesman trying to sell a pea green Yugo to a woman on Park Avenue. I always got the same response. "Give us Julie Andrews and we'd be happy to do a story on the show." What theater publication wouldn't be happy to do a piece on her? It was Julie Andrews, for God's sake. I mean, Mary fucking Poppins, the Mercedes Benz of entertainers to theater journalists. Unfortunately, I was never able to bargain using Ms. Andrews as leverage. My boss wouldn't allow it. He worked with Ms. Andrews exclusively and I wasn't allowed any contact with her. Other members of "my people" would have staged a revolt after hearing such troubling news. I viewed it as less work for me.

Instead, I was given the great fortune of working with the "day players," as I like to call them. You know, these were the actors that you'd have to give a reporter your right nut in order for them to write a small 500-word story about them. These were also the actors that demanded the most press and couldn't understand why they weren't getting a full feature in *People* magazine.

Finally, I pitched a small publication like *Entertainment Columbus* and hit pay dirt. A full two pages in their winter issue. I was ecstatic because I had successfully placed these actors, whom no one knew, in a magazine. I thought I was a miracle worker! I remembered putting all my press placements up on the wall. The other publicists had *Theater World*, *Hollywood Reporter*, and *Time* pasted on their cubicle. I had *Toronto Weekly*, *Phoenix Review*, and *Bill's Online Journal* on mine.

My very own "day player" showed up with two suitcases at my

apartment later that evening, to my horror. I had chalked up my conversation with Billy as "drunk talk." Everybody makes plans with people when they're drunk, but no one ever actually goes *through* with them. It's an unwritten rule. I thought everybody knew that. I remember telling my best friend in a drunken bonding experience that I'd give her my sperm if she ever needed it to conceive. I wouldn't expect her to show up at my front door with a Dixie cup and a stack of porn (and I'm praying she doesn't). Somehow, in my haziness, I remembered the phrase, "It'd only be for a few days, a week tops." I showed him to his new bed, my sofa, and passed out on my bed hoping it had all been just a terrible dream.

Days turned into weeks, weeks turned into months, and months turned into my mental breakdown. The allure of having an industry insider in my apartment quickly wore off when my apartment began to reek of egg farts. I was willing to overlook all of this and more simply because . . . he was a model, for God's sake! Initially, I must confess, I was quite happy to have him there. I kept telling myself that fame breeds fame, or at the very least he'd be good at bringing other hot male models to my place and just maybe I'd finally meet the man of my dreams. Billy did bring other hot men back to my apartment, but usually to have sex with him. In fact, Billy brought a lot of men in general back to my apartment, hot or not, and usually asked me to go downstairs to the diner so he could have some "private time."

Over stale grilled cheese, it didn't take long for me to find out how the beautiful people kept themselves looking great. They couch surfed so they didn't have to worry about silly things like paying for rent, electric, cable, water, groceries, and the phone bill. No, those menial things were left to us commoners.

I skipped angry and went straight to bitter. I left Billy little notes around the house reminding him that the kitchen counter was not the place to leave his dirty underwear while waiting to send it out to the cleaners. I also had to remind him to please make sure that after he'd had sex on my couch (with a man he brought to my home while I was sleeping less than three feet away), condoms don't always flush down the toilet on the first try and in the future it'd be a good idea to look to make sure it went down. I started signing my name Robert Joseph Bitterman, as in "bitter man."

I secretly longed to have such a carefree existence and sleep with as many people as he did. I couldn't for several reasons, the two primary being that a) I wasn't a model and b) I hadn't been raised to do such. My mother would break out the wooden spoon and break it over my ass had I acted so piggish. Billy, on the other hand, wasn't fazed by Mr. Bitterman at all. He thought it was a character from one of the shows I was doing the publicity for.

Billy eventually found a bigger apartment with more amenities than mine to crash at, and as bitter as I was about all his freeloading, I was sad to see him go. No matter how much I loved being around somebody who was "in the biz," living with him made me realize why I was happy being on the sidelines working at a small theater PR firm. Nobody cared what he thought or wanted his opinion. They wanted him to either look sexy, have sex, or be a nice accessory to the apartment, like a bright, beautiful new pillow on the sofa. It was the closest I ever came to becoming a starfucker— yet without the fucking.

When I was growing up, my mother would say to me, "This is your life, starring you! Make it your own." I'd usually roll my eyes and go back to watching MTV. I never quite knew or cared what she meant. Instead, I spent almost my entire life living through other people, whether it was doing shows for family members, publicizing struggling actors, or living vicariously through a sexually insatiable model. But what do you do when you realize that living your own life just isn't that interesting?

Mama Says

"Are you practicing your dance moves for the contest?" I asked Robert. It was nearly midnight on a Thursday night and we were returning Robert's call from earlier. He had been out with his temporary roommate.

"I'm not entering this year. I sprained my ankle," he said. Every year on New Year's Eve, we and our kids pretend that we're going to have a huge dance contest in the middle of our living room. We joke that the competition would be fierce, and on New Year's Day each member of the family would claim to have won even though we were all in different parts of the country. We are weird, what can I say.

I think Robert started the idea for the contest and that really was a surprise to no one. I have to say he was good; he could dance, act, and even sing. I took him all over to concerts when he was young and we always had a carload going somewhere. I think acting would have been his thing, but he never pursued it. I think it was partly because he believed his sister, who always told him he had a flat nose and no lips. She was only joking, but the poor kid believed anything she'd say.

"How's it going with the roommate?" I asked.

"Well, you know," Robert said.

"Got it," I said.

"Wait, why are you guys still awake? You're usually in bed by like six o'clock."

"Funny," I said. "We both drank too much coffee after we went to dinner." At that moment, our doorbell rang.

"Was that the door?" Robert asked.

"Hold on," I said.

Ron and I looked at each other and we nervously walked toward the door. It was late.

"Mom, don't answer the door!" Robert said.

"Your dad is already on the way to the door," I said.

"Don't! The only people out at this hour in Bloomington are serial killers and drunks," Robert said.

I saw Ron's shoulders relax and he laughed. He backed away from the door and I saw our old childhood friend Cliff Grant walk inside.

"It's Cliff Grant," I said into the phone.

"Oh. I got the drunk part right, at least," Robert said.

"Robert!" I smiled at Cliff walking into my kitchen.

"Sorry, Mom, every time he stays with you guys he's wasted. I'm sure he's going to ask to stay for at least a week or two. Isn't that his usual MO?"

"Let me call you in the morning," I said.

"Byeeeee," Robert said, mocking me.

I went into our living room and sat down on the sofa and listened to Cliff and Ron talk. He was passing through town and stopped for a business dinner and he thought he'd stop by and say hello despite the late hour. Cliff always had a hard time dealing with the fact that he was no longer seventeen and in high school. He always talked about the good old days and quite frankly never had better days than the ones he had at school with Ron and me. He often would stay with us for a week or two at a time while he was looking for work when the kids were younger. I was still surprised that he was at our house so late at night. Maybe Robert was right. Maybe he wasn't only a drunk, but also a serial killer? But at the moment, the drunk was overpowering the killer.

Cliff went on and on about how wonderful it was that Ron and I were still together after so many years and how our friendship throughout the years was one of his most cherished. Since his divorce over ten years ago, life hadn't been so good, he explained. He lost his job, he spent all of his money, and no longer had a big house.

He went on to tell us that his current girlfriend was not happy that he had moved back in with his mother. He felt like she was going to break up with him at any moment because of his living situation. Cliff was aghast how people could be so petty and judgmental.

"And Michael? He's married with children, right?"

I smiled and nodded.

"Such a gift from God," Cliff said. "And how about the little troublemaker Julie? She's doing well? She has children, too, yes?"

"Yes, I wouldn't have called her a troublemaker but yes, she's married with kids and is a schoolteacher now. We get up to visit her and the kids a few times a year," I explained. I wondered how much longer these niceties were going to go on. It was nearly twelve thirty and I was ready for bed. I kept thinking either ask to stay or go, but don't keep us awake any longer. This old lady was tired.

Cliff clearly had been to a bar before that, as I could smell the rum. As he talked to Ron about the days when he would babysit Michael and Julie, I felt my eyes growing heavier. I was about to bite the bullet and ask him if he wanted to stay in our guest room when he turned to me and said, "Oh, and I heard about Robert."

"What do you mean?" I asked.

"Jane Ann," he said, like I was back in high school.

I had a feeling where he was going with the conversation so instead of playing coy, I went the direct route. "That he came out?"

"Uh, yes," Cliff said.

"We're proud of our son, and all of our kids," I said nonchalantly. I put the invitation to stay the night on hold.

"It's just hard to believe that he chose that way of life," he said and shook his head. He then shrugged in disgust and crinkled his face. I cocked my head back in surprise. Invitation revoked.

"Are you okay?" I asked, referring to his facial expression and the gagging motions he made.

"I don't particularly agree with the lifestyle," Cliff said.

"I'm sorry, what?" I said.

"The gay lifestyle. I don't agree with it," he said.

"Cliff, it's not really something you agree or disagree with—it just is. It would be like you were saying 'I don't agree with your blue eyes, Jane.' It's something you're born with and like my blue eyes, it doesn't define you as a person, but it is a part of you."

"Jane, it's not heredity. You and Ron shouldn't blame yourselves. He made that choice. It's an illness," he said. My mouth dropped and I could feel my face getting warmer.

"I can see you're getting upset," Cliff said.

"I'm not upset. I'm just really confused," I said, obviously lying about my anger. I looked at Ron for support.

"Do you know any gay people, Cliff?" Ron asked.

"No, I don't. But I can tell you this, my son Derek was recently in New York visiting a friend. They went out to the bars and Derek got separated from the group. He was talking to a girl and you know how that goes . . ."

"Yes, Cliff, we know how that goes," I interrupted.

He chuckled at this. "Anyway, he found himself walking around the gay neighborhood, Chelsea. Derek said all these men kept staring at him and he was worried that one of them was going to get him."

I burst into laughter.

"What?" he asked.

"Get him? Really?" I asked.

"It's not uncommon for gay men to prey upon a young good-looking twenty-three-year-old."

"What are you talking about?" Ron asked.

"I'm sorry, how is that different from any other man or woman when they see a good-looking twenty-three-year-old?" I asked, attempting to lighten the mood.

"No, this was very different. It was late at night. He was worried that one of these men would try and rape him," Cliff said. "Gay men are known to be very predatory."

"Okay, I've had . . ." I started.

"Oh, come on," Ron interrupted. "We've gone to gay places many, many times and never once felt that."

"But Ron, no offense, you're older. It's not like you're Derek's age and men would be after you," Cliff said.

"Trust me, Cliff, heads turned when Ron walked into places. I still don't understand your thought process," I said.

"I will say that I was relieved that Derek made it out of that neighborhood safely," he said.

"Well, I think I'm going to go to bed," I announced.

Ron looked at me and knew immediately that I was done. "Yes, it's getting late," Ron said.

"Oh, so I guess I'm going?" Cliff asked.

"Yeah, it's probably best you get on the road before it gets any later. You've got another hour and a half drive. You don't want to fall asleep at the wheel," Ron said.

I stood in the doorway and Cliff walked toward me.

"It was nice to see you, Jane. I hope you're not angry. I do believe it's a choice or some type of mental illness there," he said.

I stayed silent, trying my best not to say something that I would later regret. He walked to the front door with Ron.

"Cliff?" I said, not able to stay quiet.

"Yes?" he asked.

"Did you ever think that maybe Derek is gay?" I said.

"Never," he said matter-of-factly.

"Okay," I said. "But what if he was? Anything is possible."

Cliff was at a loss for words. I wasn't trying to imply that his son was gay. I had no way of knowing, but I wanted him to put himself in my shoes for even one second. He refused.

"Good night, Cliff."

Cliff didn't say a word and walked to his car. Ron shut the door behind him and to this day we've never heard from our "lifelong" friend again.

CHAPTER EIGHTEEN

You Don't Need Therapy; You're Just Hungry

The phrase commonly used by my mother when I mention
I'm seeing a therapist

There are just certain things you do in New York that you don't do in the Midwest. You ride the subways. You compliment the trannie hookers on their shoes when getting your Sunday *New York Times*. You walk six blocks and four avenues over to go to the gym, but you'll have a six-pack of Diet Coke delivered from the deli downstairs because you don't feel like walking. Finally, you go to therapy. Why? Because everyone else does, and you don't want to be the maladjusted one left behind.

My mother, on the other hand, holds the belief that Manhattanites' biggest and toughest emotional problems can be resolved with one thing: food.

"You're going to spend a hundred and fifty dollars to sit in some stranger's office for an hour so he can blame your father and me for all your problems? That makes a lot of sense. Here, let me cut to the chase: We screwed you up. Now give me a hundred bucks."

After I failed to show her the benefits of psychotherapy, she continued. "I'm giving you a discount. What more do you want from me?"

During my cab ride to my therapist's office on the Upper West Side, I began to tally just how much I'd spent on my counseling sessions—$150 per session, or $300 a month. (I was considered one of the "less fortunate" by Manhattan standards, as I could only afford to see my therapist every other week.)

For an extra $300 a month, I could have afforded an apartment slightly larger than the shoebox I was in, possibly an apartment with another room. (How exciting!) For three hundred bucks I could have bought a round-trip ticket to Miami Beach for the weekend on one of those discount Web sites. I imagined myself poolside at the Delano Hotel while I sat in my therapist's waiting room.

I glanced at my watch and counted the minutes while I waited for my doc to invite me in. With every minute that passed, I grew angrier. I took out my cell phone and began to calculate how much he was making off of me. Exactly $3.33 per minute. The psychic hotlines gave more definitive advice in about half the time. Hell, a hooker would have been less, or at least so I'd heard.

I was fuming, as he was now running five minutes late and I no doubt would be charged for the time that *he* was late. I'd just given him $16.67 for absolutely nothing. I had eaten leftover pizza for a week so I could let my neuroses explode in the comfort of a therapist's office, and here he was acting as if five minutes was nothing. How dare this asshole be so blasé with my money! That could have been a movie ticket and a bottle of water for me. It was a wasted cheese-burger deluxe meal at the Fifty-eighth Street diner. With every passing minute, my mother's voice resonated in my ear: "Take the hundred and fifty dollars you're spending at the therapist's and have a nice dinner with a few friends. Have a session where you can just vent." My mother hasn't had a single therapy session in her life, and suddenly she was leagues above Dr. Morty. "Trust me, you'll feel much better, and you'll at least have something to show for it after-wards," she said, interrupting my own stream of consciousness.

The clock continued to click and still no doc. I remembered my last trip back home and how refreshed I'd felt when I returned back to the chaotic life of New York. Typically, I went to visit my par-ents for a long weekend in what I call my very own "Betty Ford Clinic." Not that I was addicted to drugs or had a drinking prob-lem (unless you called weekend apple martinis a problem), but when I went back to the Midwest, I was allowed to slow down and let my body decompress, which I couldn't do in New York. The only problem was, I didn't know how to do it anymore.

Living in a small town in Middle America, there are only so many things you can do for fun. Having walked around my town's two malls twice, made my annual pilgrimage to Target (pronounced TAR-JAY by the upper class), worked out at the new gym, and cruised the college campus to look at the cute college boys, there wasn't much left to do, and that was all before eleven. Thankfully, my father suggested one of my family's favorite pastimes, riverboat gambling.

For most people, going to a smoke-filled boat where people drink vodka and orange juice at nine o'clock in the morning and bet their mortgage payments in the span of thirty minutes wouldn't exactly be a place of family togetherness. For my parents and me, there was no better way to bond. Some call riverboat gambling a path straight to hell; I call it family therapy for bored Midwesterners.

This floating casino offered us glowing lights, the buzz of slot machines, the cashing of chips, and ladies with big hair. Small communities could be found nestled inside their Aqua-Net infused hair. Forty minutes later, I was seated at the blackjack table in between my mother and my father.

You can learn a lot about your family members at a blackjack table. My mother plays with the $300 my father gives her. Much to her credit, he never realizes that whether she wins or loses, she pilfers her chips and puts them in her purse when he is focused on splitting eights. "I'm going to be wishing I had that three hundred dollars next week," she laments after she loses a hand while sliding a $25 chip into her purse under the table. After years of playing, I know her game and go along with it; however, these days I usually ask for a percentage. My therapist would say that my mother is clearly trying to establish financial independence from the rest of the family. My mother would argue that she simply wants the three hundred for a few pairs of shoes and some DKNY perfume from Bergner's.

My father's greatest joy playing blackjack is to give advice to my mother and me on every hand we play (even though I've been playing blackjack in casinos since I was seventeen, thanks to my mother). Halfway through our time at the casino, no matter who is seated, he tells the table of cranky middle-aged (and mostly male) gamblers that I'm his son visiting from New York, as if they should be excited to be seated next to genuine "city folk." This exciting tidbit is usually met with a glare or the occasional cigarette smoke blown in my face. My therapist concluded that my father is an alpha male who seeks validation of his youngest son from the rest of society, since the son has not quite reached the level of greatness of his father. My mother, on the contrary, would say that he's just making conversation.

While the three of us sat quietly at the table waiting to make our fortune, our dealer, Keshawn, told me she had big dreams of leaving the Riverboat Empire behind and moving to a big city to do hair. "I bet you have a lot of girlfriends in New York," she said sweetly.

I smiled. "No, not really," I said, focusing on my hand, debating whether I should take a hit on sixteen.

"Oh, come on. You're a very handsome guy. I bet you have to beat them off with a stick," she flirted.

Just as I was about to give what would no doubt be an utterly charming response, my mother interrupted from the other side of the table, "No, but he does have a lot of *guys* chasing him." My father spit his Diet Pepsi all over the dumbfounded blackjack dealer and the table. Poor Keshawn. All she did was try to make pleasant conversation, but instead, my mother outed me to her. She stood facing us with Diet Pepsi dripping from her name tag. The man to my left took another puff of his cigarette and sat unaffected, while the man to my dad's right shook his head in disbelief and moved his chair farther away from me as we waited for the cleaners to steam vac the table.

The game finally resumed on the same hand that had been interrupted, thanks to my mother, and it was now my play. "Hit me," I said to the dealer as her eyes bulged at this latest piece of news to the blackjack table.

"Bust!" she said with a slight twinge of happiness in her voice. Suddenly, the table began to turn for the worse. Where do you go from there? I couldn't leave the table, not because I was worried I'd be thought of as a wimp, but because it was the middle of the shoe and you can't leave once you've started. I tried to catch my mother's eye to stare her down, but she knew better than to look my way. My dad continued to stare at his cards as if he was in the World Championships. I, on the other hand, suddenly found myself "butching" it up for the rest of the table.

I consider myself a very masculine guy as it is, but in this environment I felt like I needed to overcompensate. When the cocktail waitress passed offering to replace my bottle of water with another, I grabbed her elbow and said in a Bronx accent, "I'll take a Corona." For some reason, I thought sounding like a thug would make the rest of the table forget about my sexuality. My father and mother simultaneously stared at me with that you–were–born–in–Illinois–not–in–one–of–the–five–boroughs look.

"Corona?" the waitress questioned.

"Yeah, Corona, why?" I rebuffed. She shrugged her shoulders and retreated to her station. I didn't know what I'd said that was so offensive. I was simply trying to be one of the guys. I looked at my watch and realized it was only ten in the morning.

My father would later tell me in the parking lot that if I was trying to look like a tough guy, I shouldn't order a Corona. Apparently, it was a girl's beer to manly men in the Midwest. With a stash of cash in my pocket and a buzz from the one beer on an empty stomach, I rode home nauseous with my mother in my ear, telling me she didn't understand the problem with telling Keshawn I was gay. If I was "a gay," as she once again said, I should be "a proud gay."

Back in my therapist's office, I sat thinking of my riverboat gambling experience packed with self-discovery and proclamations. All in all, I ended up winning $600 that day and managed to make a few self-discoveries, particularly that I wasn't as comfortable with discussing my sexuality as I thought. So I wondered what exactly I was doing sitting in Dr. Morty's office paying him to be late. I was furious. I was mad at him for being so late. I was mad at my mother for telling the blackjack dealer I was gay. I was even more pissed at myself for letting the two of them bother me.

My therapist finally opened the door a full fourteen minutes late (or $46.66, depending on how you look at it). I was seething mad.

"You look a little upset today, Robert," Dr. Morty observed. I was so glad my money was being well spent on this genius. "What seems to be the problem?" he asked as I sat in the cushy leather armchair. I wanted to tell him that I felt ripped off that I had been left waiting for the last fourteen minutes while he took his sweet time. I wanted to tell him that I really didn't see the point of our visits anymore. I wanted to scream at him for every time I asked what he thought I should do and he responded with, "What do you think you should do?" I wanted to tell him that he was useless. I wanted to tell him that at $150 for forty-five minutes, he should have solved all of my problems while serving me a double espresso.

"Well," I said confidently. I paused and then blurted out uncontrollably, "My mother thinks this therapy thing is a complete waste of time and I should take my money elsewhere."

Needless to say, he thought my mother's idea was elementary

and borderline infantile. When my mother called the next morning, I let her know what Dr. Morty had said, thus setting up a feud greater than Cher and Bette, or Christina and Britney, and somehow each week at therapy I wound up right smack dab in the middle of it.

Mama Says

I'm not against therapy. Believe me, there are a lot of people who need it for one reason or another, and I do believe some people have chemical imbalances. I have family members who are therapists, and now, in addition to being a teacher, my daughter is a counselor. So, as you see, I am not opposed to them. However, we live in a society filled with people flocking to therapy when things are going slightly less than perfect in their lives. We're quick to dispense a handful of cash to a person with three letters after their name in hopes that they'll have the answer to the puzzle. Does that really ever help anyone? Sure, you might make small gains and get some insight. Let me put it into terms most gay men can relate to: If you are working out and you grab a dumbbell that is slightly difficult for you to lift, are you making any great strides? If you grab the heavier one, the one that you know will take more time to master, wouldn't you be getting more from it? Life isn't easy, and I'm not against asking for help, but whatever happened to working through it yourself?

I had a friend who signed up for therapy because she felt that her husband was going to leave her for another woman. She'd been happily married for nineteen years and her husband had given her no indication of wanting out, nor did she have a reason to suspect he was cheating. Instead, she signed up for therapy in the event that he *might* leave her one day. I remember her telling me, "I just want to be prepared for everything, just in case. You just never know these days." I fear a lot of things. I worry about biological terrorism, but I don't walk around in a Hazmat suit.

Let the life event happen first is my opinion. Then, if you feel like you need to talk to someone about it, go for it, but don't put the carriage before the horse. Sometimes, I think all it takes is for a friend to sit you down and give you a good smack on the back of the head while shouting, "Snap out of it, you moron!"

I just don't understand this mentality, and sadly my friend isn't the only "therapaholic" I know. I just didn't realize it was so close to home.

We sat down to dinner every night as a family, whether the kids liked it or not. Everyone's issues were laid out right then and there over roast beef and mashed potatoes. Someone at the table always had something traumatic happen to them on a daily basis. With the rest of the family around us, a pearl of wisdom was bound to be shed, even if it came through a mouthful of potatoes. There were a total of five different perspectives at one table—pick the one that worked best for your situation and that felt right in your heart. Therefore, I was quite surprised to learn that Robert was going to therapy.

After Robert dropped this latest bombshell, I ran to the grocery store to pick up a few things and to stew a little about my son going to therapy. I charged down the aisles with my shopping cart, making my way through the bakery section like a woman betrayed. I went around the corners and vented to myself. Was he talking about me? Was his therapist saying that I had screwed him up? Damn him. I felt guilty at first. I thought maybe we didn't let him know enough that we didn't care if he was gay, but he assured me he was doing fine in that department. What could it be, then? It was driving me insane.

I found myself in the paper products aisle staring blankly at rows of toilet paper and paper towels. I wasn't shopping for either; I was trying to figure out what in the hell that little shit was saying about his father and me in that therapy session.

I felt a tap on my shoulder that startled me, setting off a chain reaction and scaring the older woman who tapped me on the shoulder. I must have looked like a woman possessed. I quickly apologized and went back to staring at toilet paper. Then the woman, in her early seventies, looked at me very seriously and said, "Miss?" At first I didn't hear her, as I was imagining Robert sitting in his therapist's chair. "Excuse me, miss," she repeated.

"Yes?" I said, thinking she was going to ask me if I was all right, since I probably looked deranged by this point.

"What kind of toilet paper do you use?" she asked.

"I'm sorry. What did you say?"

She repeated, "What kind of toilet paper do you use?"

I paused for a moment and then said, "Well, I like White Cloud the best, I suppose."

"My brand always sticks," she proceeded to tell me.

"I'm sorry to hear that," I said, as if my brain had been on a satellite delay. It was beyond surreal. I began to laugh. I handed her a four-pack of White Cloud and told her to try it, that it would help get rid of her "sticking" problem. She then threw her arms around me, hugged me, and thanked me. She walked away without saying another word, and I stood there dumbfounded, once again staring at the rows of toilet paper.

The rest of my time at the grocery store I found myself laughing one minute and full of introspection the next. It was bizarre. I saw the woman again in the checkout lane with only one person in between us. She smiled and nodded at me but never said another word. We had bonded, sisters of toilet tissue. She left and I made my way to the cashier and we both glanced at the woman as she was leaving. "Such a nice lady," I said.

"Yeah, she's so sweet. She just lost her husband a few months ago. He always used to do the shopping with her. It's gotta be tough." The cashier sighed as she continued to ring me up.

During the drive home, I began to think about Robert. I was obsessed with my son's therapy because of what it meant to *me*, not him. I laughed at the woman in the grocery store because she embarrassed *me*. I felt horrible. I'd ignored both of their feelings, when the truth was that they were reflecting *my* insecurities. I called Robert when I got home, took a deep breath, and asked him about his therapy session. I listened, trying not to view his therapy as a reflection of my failures as a mother. It's like they say: If you don't learn from your mistakes, there's no sense making them.

I never quite realized the impact of talking to a stranger about everyday things and the power it has to change your entire perspective. Now I try to be in the paper aisle alone whenever I can. People tend to open up to me all the time. I'm very quiet and a bit shy, so it seems funny that people are drawn to me when they wish to share their life's events, even if it is just toilet paper.

Who knows? Maybe if we all had someone to talk over life's ups and downs with, we would all be better off. You know, now that I think about it, maybe I need a therapist, too.

CHAPTER NINETEEN

When Jane Met Gidget

A Little Girl, with Big Ideas; well, little nonetheless

My ex-boyfriend and I were physically and culturally complete opposites. I'm a white boy from the Midwest with light hair and eyes. He's an Italian tough guy from Queens with dark hair and beautiful brown eyes. I was in shape and occasionally went to the gym when I could muster the energy. I figured since I had a boyfriend, I could put the single man's body to the back of the closet. He, on the other hand, would get up at six every morning, trot off to the gym, work out for ninety minutes, and return home looking like an ad for *Men's Health*. I was six years younger than him, a fact that I reveled in with the passing of every birthday. He, on the other hand, snarled when I reminded him of this. Like most polite Midwesterners, I rarely argued, and shut down emotionally when conflict arose. He could argue better than any lawyer I knew and wasn't afraid to tell me exactly how he was feeling when he was feeling it. I loved watching college basketball. He loved playing bocce ball. I said things like, "How do you like them apples?" and "He's a day late and a dollar short." He responded to the same situations with phrases like, "Get the fuck out of here" and "He's sweatin' like a whore in church." Different in almost every conceivable way, that was pretty much us. But it worked.

Rocco and I bought a place together after a little over a year of dating. Buying a place with someone is scary enough; buying a place in Manhattan early on in a relationship is terrifying and frankly can be a deal breaker. At first, we didn't see eye to eye on what kind of apartment we wanted. Pre-war? One or two bed-room? Traditional? Contemporary? Thankfully, we had both de-cided that we wanted to live in the West Village. So you can imagine my surprise when Rocco came back one Sunday afternoon and informed me that he had made an offer on a place . . . in Midtown. I hated Midtown. It was crowded and touristy. But I loved my boy-friend and he loved the apartment so much that I wasn't about to pee on his parade. Yes, buying a place was a leap of faith, but it was one that we both were ready to make.

One person who was particularly happy about this latest devel-opment was my mom. She usually tried to find any excuse possible for a trip to New York, and our new apartment was a good enough reason. Even though my dad couldn't come because of work there was no keeping my mother home. Growing up, we used to joke that she had a bag packed at all times in case the opportunity to travel arose. At least I thought it was a joke, until one day I was get-ting a towel out of the hall closet and discovered a duffel bag full of my mom's things. She wasn't playing around. This woman was like a refugee ready to fly the coop at a moment's notice. Then again, with my father's incessant snoring, who could blame her?

A visit from my mother wasn't unusual. However, her coming to visit me for the first time that I was living with my boyfriend in our new place was a very big deal to me. For some reason, it triggered every neurotic bone in my body. I wanted her visit to be perfect. She'd stayed at my place many times and I didn't stress one bit, but I guess in retrospect Rocco and I acted like any married couple does who has family coming to visit.

My mom was due to arrive on Saturday in the early afternoon. The night before, Rocco and I went to dinner with friends and got back home around one in the morning. Not too bad, I thought. I'd get a couple of hours of sleep, get up, run to Starbucks, do the laundry, run to the grocery store, and pick up some of my mom's favorite things. I set my alarm for seven thirty.

Or at least I thought I did.

The next morning, I opened my eyes and peacefully stared out the window. I took a deep breath, exhaled, and then smiled. This was pretty amazing. I was an openly gay man living with my boyfriend and we were having my mom in for the weekend. In all my years of living a closeted life, I'd never imagined that this was even a possibility. But here it was, a reality. I stood up to go brush my teeth and glanced at the alarm clock on Rocco's nightstand.

"Holy shit!" I shouted.

Rocco shot up like the house was engulfed in flames. "WHAT'S WRONG?" He had two Cheerios stuck to the side of his face. There was no time to ask why he was eating Cheerios in bed, but I made a mental note to revisit that issue later. Did he have some sort of weird sleep eating problem that I didn't know about?

"It's almost ten o'clock! Her flight lands in three hours," I yelled at him.

"What?" he said and furrowed his brow.

"Where's the housekeeper? I thought she was coming at nine. You know her. You have to call her right now, Rocco. This is not good. This is not good at all." I grabbed his phone off the nightstand and threw it on the bed.

"Ten o'clock? Shit, I have to be to work in thirty minutes," he said in a gravelly voice.

"Yes, Rocco, it's ten o'clock! Hello?" I said.

Still half asleep, Rocco grumbled something at me as I ran out of the room.

I found the phone number for our occasional housekeeper, Eva, and left her several frantic messages. I calmed myself down long enough to start prepping for the cleaning lady's arrival. I tidied up a bit, but mainly I downed a double shot of espresso and made a gigantic list for her to accomplish over the course of four hours. I went to the computer and prayed that my mom's flight was running late. After punching in her flight number, I was horrified to learn that it was arriving forty minutes early.

I started with the laundry, washing the sheets in the guest bedroom even though no one had used it in over six months. I put fresh towels and toilet paper in the guest bath. I was ready for Eva to arrive so we could get down to business.

I shouted to Rocco from the kitchen, "Eva may hate me before the day is over." *Okay, hate me even more.* "I'm apologizing to her in advance when she gets here. Do you have an extra fifty bucks we can give to her so she doesn't stab me with a kitchen knife after she sees my list?"

In the midst of my prep work, I didn't see Rocco walk into the kitchen holding his toothbrush.

"Where's our toothpaste?" he asked.

"Oh, I put it in the guest bathroom for my mom. I didn't make it to CVS yet," I explained. "Why?"

Rocco held up his toothbrush and said, "I want to let you know that I brushed my teeth for a good minute and a half before noticing something was different. I thought maybe you switched toothpaste brands or that maybe it was a new flavor. Then I realized that I was brushing with Preparation H."

"I think you're looking for blame. I'm not to blame. You should have looked at the tube before just haphazardly placing it on your toothbrush," I said.

"I was still half asleep. It was where our toothpaste has been every day for the last four months," he said. "I'm going to be at work all day tasting hemorrhoid cream. Thank you for that." He went back to the bedroom and no doubt scoured his mouth with some sort of disinfectant as he got ready for work.

I quickly forgot about the hemorrhoid incident and could only focus on the fact that Rocco had to go into work, thereby freeing him of any preparation for my mother's arrival. That was a tough pill to swallow, probably like the Preparation H that was on Rocco's toothbrush. However, I talked myself out of being pissed about it since it was *my* mother coming to visit. I knew which skeletons of mine needed to be tucked deeply into our bedroom closet and how to hide them from a nosy mother. However, Rocco was a different story.

Rocco got dressed in a flash and was out the door, but not before hugging me good-bye and reassuring me that everything was going to be fine. Or as he put it, "Calm the hell down."

When Eva finally showed I didn't have time for niceties and to be honest she really didn't like me all that much. To start her off on the right note, I handed her the to-do list and an extra fifty bucks.

"What's this?" she asked.

"It's from Rocco."

Her eyes lit up and she said, "He's such a giving man. He doesn't need to give me extra. Why would he do that?" she asked in a flirty tone as if he had left a love note for me to pass on to her.

"It's for whatever awful things may come out of my mouth in the next two hours. Now let's get moving." Her smile quickly faded. She was instantly pissed and I hadn't even been allowed to have a meltdown. I had blown it already.

An hour later, Rocco called to check on me from work.

"'Sup, babe?" he asked.

"Eva showed up an hour ago, but she's moving like a turtle on Ambien. She hates me. And you know exactly why! This is your fault." Eva had been Rocco's housekeeper before we met. She did everything for him right down to folding his underwear. She had a not-so-secret crush on him and saw me as the roadblock to their happiness. When Rocco and I moved in together, Eva was blatantly curt with me. In fact, she didn't say anything to me the first three times she came to the apartment. I thought she didn't speak English until Rocco told me that she was born in Riverside.

"It's all on me. I've been dusting the shelves and cleaning the kitchen. I swear to God it's like we are Big Edie and Little Edie living at Grey Gardens for Christ's sake. I mean, obviously, you're Big Edie since you're older than me."

"What? Who the fuck is Big Edie? Yes, I know I'm older than you, dipshit. Lay off the caffeine," Rocco said.

"I think I should open a bottle of wine to calm my nerves."

"It's eleven thirty," he said.

"Don't judge me! You're not here!" I barked like a crazy person.

"Because I'm at work. Rob, you just need to relax. Stop cleaning. Go outside. Run to the deli, buy some fresh flowers or something. Have an espresso. Get a cookie. Do something. Honestly, I don't get the anxiety. It's your mother, not a march on Washington."

The ironic part was that *I* typically was the voice of reason. I was the one that calmed Rocco down. So much so, in fact, that he would often introduce me to friends or co-workers as "my Xanax, Rob." It was cute in a way that only an anti-depressant could possibly be. However, I appreciated that Rocco was trying to be *my* anti-anxiety medication at that moment, but I was like a junkie that no pill would satiate.

"I realize this is not a march on Washington and I'm not trying to attempt some grand political statement about gays and lesbians, Rocco. But I am trying to show my Midwestern mother that we are like every other married couple and that we don't walk around the house in a pair of women's six-inch heels all day long."

"Heels? What are you talking about?"

"You've seen the stereotypes on TV," I said.

"Yes, but your mother . . ."

"Which reminds me, by the way, have you thrown out those

shoes your friends Dave and Eddie left here when they did drag for Halloween?" I interrupted. "I don't need my mother discovering them in some closet when we're out of the house and then whispering about it when she's on the phone with my dad."

Fortunately, Rocco knew that when I got into one of my neurotic fits it was best to just let me roll. I'm sure it took every last ounce of his Italian blood not to say anything to me. "Rob, they are just a pair of shoes. And come on, your mom would know that you have better taste in women's shoes than the ones that were left here," Rocco said and started to laugh.

"Are you kid—"

"Who friggin' cares? I was only asking why you're stressing out so much about this," Rocco interrupted.

"Honestly, Rocco, I think having high heels in the house is seriously ridiculous. But if that's the message you want to send to my mother, go right ahead. Maybe we can ask Sherry Vine and Lady Bunny to have dinner with us, too, Rocco. Better yet, they can give me a full drag queen makeover for my mom. I can lip-sync to Patti LaBelle in our living room. How about that? What would my drag name even be? Have you thought about that? Roberta Rhinestones? What would it be, Rocco? Come on. I'm waiting."

"How about 'Crazy Pants'?" Rocco said before he hung up.

Normally, that would have infuriated me, but Rocco was right. He didn't need to know that bit of information, but he was.

Thirty minutes later there was a knock on my front door. For a moment, I thought it was my mother and panicked, but I quickly realized I had roughly two, *maybe* two and a half, hours left to spare depending on whether or not she checked a bag. It was the doorman with a package from FedEx. He handed me a fairly large box addressed to Rocco and me.

"Sorry. I'm crazed right now," I said and snatched the box out of his hand and quickly shut the door. When I raced back into the

Robert Rave and Jane Rave

house to continue cleaning, I suddenly realized the apartment was strangely quiet. What the hell was Eva doing? She'd been in the same bathroom for almost forty minutes and hadn't come out.

"Eva?" I yelled.

No answer. I walked down into the center of the living room and tried again.

"Eva? Hello? Is everything okay in there? Do you feel okay?" I said. I heard a soda can open. "I know you can hear me." With that, the vacuum immediately powered on so that she could drown out my voice. Hey, if it got her moving faster, I wasn't about to be insulted.

I decided that I was going to open the bottle of Riesling we had in our fridge. When I turned to walk back to the kitchen, I was greeted with an unexpected surprise.

"Hi. What are you doing here?" I asked.

"I took the day off. I had Valerie reschedule my appointments. I thought you could use the help," Rocco said. What kind of lottery did I win to deserve this man? I went and hugged him tightly.

"I'm calmer already," I said and smiled. "Thank you."

"What's that box in the kitchen?" Rocco asked.

"I don't know, I got distracted by your girlfriend Eva. Could you please do something to light a fire under her ass? She's not listening to me."

"Because she knows who's the boss," he said.

"Cute," I said.

Rocco walked to the kitchen and grabbed the FedEx box and pulled out a note.

"Hey, it's from Ms. X," he said and flashed a devilish smile.

Ms. X is a pop star that shall forever remain nameless. No, really, it's in both my best interest and hers that her identity never be revealed. All that you need to know is that she's gorgeous and incredibly talented. Beyond that, I really can't say much more without revealing who she is. Also, she's got a lot of dirt on me that I don't want her unearthing when she decides to write her own book. Therefore, she'll remain Ms. X.

Ms. X and I had become friends shortly before Rocco and I started dating. In fact, the first time she met Rocco at a group dinner she pulled him aside and told him that if he hurt me in any way, shape, or form that she knew "people." These were the kind of "people" that only heads of state, crime bosses, and pop stars knew. I watched the conversation from a few feet away as I hailed a cab. I knew what she was up to; she had told me she was going to have a talk with him. When their conversation ended, Ms. X said goodbye to our other dinner companions and Rocco walked over and stood beside me.

As we stared down Greenwich Avenue, I asked, "How'd that go?"

"I told her that I knew people, too. And her people were probably some of my distant relatives."

"Okay, then, I'm dating a Soprano."

Ms. X loved Rocco's fire and his twisted sense of humor. They became partners in crime almost immediately. So much so that when the two of them were together in the same room, their naughtiness took center stage and finding new and innovative ways of embarrassing me were Acts I, II, and III.

So you can imagine my trepidation when Rocco told me the package was from Ms. X.

"Well, what does the note say?" I asked.

Hello boys,

I saw this in the store and immediately thought of the two of you. Now, the question is, will you think of me when you're enjoying it? Be sure to let me know.

Xoxo,
Ms. X

Rocco peeked into the box and gasped. He quickly closed it and looked at me, trying his best not to laugh. Uh-oh. This was worse than I thought.

"What's in the box?"

Rocco couldn't hold it in and started giggling like a toddler. "Don't you worry about the box."

"No, seriously. What's in the box?" I asked again.

"Nothing. Well, something. Never mind, I'll show it to you later," Rocco said, and by this time he couldn't control his laughter.

"The box was addressed to me. Come on, what's in the box?" I said.

"She got us on this one," Rocco said with the kind of laugh that was typically reserved for people on hallucinogenics.

"This is not the movie *Seven*. And Gwyneth's head is not in the box. So quit playing games and just give me the box," I said, reaching for it.

"I promise, I'll show it to you later," he said.

"Rocco, show it to me. I'm wasting time here when I could be cleaning. Now just show it to me already or I will shave off half of your eyebrow when you're sleeping," I said.

"You wouldn't!"

"Try me," I said.

Before we met, Rocco once had part of his eyebrow shaved off after he passed out from a night of debauchery. He's never gotten over it and has been a light sleeper ever since. I knew this phobia and used it to my advantage. Isn't that what relationships are for?

"Rob, trust me. I'll show it to you later," he said.

Rocco's eyes momentarily moved from me to the back of the apartment and I lunged for the box. He tightened his grasp and we played a split-second game of tug-of-war, resulting in the box ripping open, sending its entire contents out onto our hardwood floors.

"What in the?" I said and quickly put my hand over my mouth.

Spilled out all over my beautiful hardwood floors were several tiny bottles of lubricant in various flavors: coconut, strawberry, banana. It was like a gelato shop, only for lube. As I turned my head slightly to the left I saw a large white towel and a smaller one that looked exactly the same. I wasn't quite sure what the joke was there until I grabbed them and saw writing on the smaller one. *Oh. My. God. She didn't.* Written on the small towel was "cum rag" and, sure enough, on the larger one, "cum towel."

As if that wasn't enough, lying next to Rocco's foot was a porn movie. But this wasn't just any porn, this movie starred "Gidget the Midget." Yes, that's right, midget porn.

"Gidget the Midget?" I said to myself. "Midget porn? She had to have been drunk to send us this. Is it politically correct to say midget porn? I mean, clearly, Ms. Gidget the Midget doesn't seem to mind." I noticed that Rocco was unusually quiet. "Hello? Are you listening?"

I looked up at Rocco and followed his eye line directly to a horrified Eva, who was staring at the mini sex shop on our living room floor.

"Oh, this isn't ours," I quickly said. "It's a gag gift."

Eva glared at me and then shook her head at Rocco. "Disgusting," she said. "I can't look at this. I'm going to be sick."

"No! You can't! My mother's going to be here very soon," I said, snapping back into panic mode.

Rocco collected the rest of Ms. X's gift from me, put it back in the box, and set it on the table. "Why don't you go get a coffee and pick up the rest of the things you needed from D'Agostino's?"

"What about the rest of the stuff that needs to be done here?" I asked.

"Eva and I will take care of it," Rocco said, doing his best to calm my nerves.

"Really? Are you sure?" I asked suspiciously.

"Yes, I got this," he said.

I grabbed my keys and made a dash for the elevator. The minute the elevator doors shut and I knew for certain that I was out of earshot I burst into laughter.

I walked outside feeling like I had a new lease on life, and I took this new lease right into the Starbucks that was located less than a hundred feet from my building. Who needed fresh air in Central Park to relax when you could smell coffee grounds mixed with lots of bad perfume? I wish I had an explanation, but I just felt some sort of gravitational pull to go inside. Plus, I was frankly too tired to do anything else. My energy had been shot in all of my panic.

The line was incredibly long, but I was surprisingly okay with it. It was time spent out of the apartment and a distraction from the ticking clock that was my mother. One thing I typically do to distract myself when I'm in these types of situations is watch other people. For example, I've never understood why when people are standing in line to purchase something they don't have either their purse open with their wallet out or cash in hand when ordering. I don't get the surprised expression on their faces. *What? I have to pay for this? It's not free? Oh, okay. Let me see if I have any money to give to you.* These people make me want to stab myself. The woman that stood in front of me was one of these people. I reached into my pocket to pull out my wallet and all I found was two crumpled singles that were left over from the cab ride the night before. In all the commotion with the gift that Ms. X sent, I didn't bother to take my wallet or my ID. Going back into my apartment was not an option. I chose the only thing I could find on the menu that I could afford. After the woman in front of me recovered from the shock of paying for her coffee, I grabbed my double espresso and immediately snagged an empty table at the back. This was a rare commodity at Starbucks, especially one in touristy Midtown.

As I sat at the tiny table, I wondered what to do next. I didn't bring my cell phone. I had no extra money to buy a *New York Times*. My espresso would take maybe thirty seconds to drink. I leaned my head against the wall. I would sit here for just a few minutes. Nearly an hour later, I felt a tap on my shoulder from a homeless man who asked to use the other chair at my table. I gave him the table and decided it was time to go home.

I walked into the apartment and it was immaculate—almost as if it were out of a movie set. We were no longer *Grey Gardens*. This thrilled me beyond words. What was even better was that Rocco handed me a large glass of vodka and soda. "I thought you could probably use this," he said and smiled.

"Yes, is Eva gone?" I asked. "She's not hiding somewhere with a knife ready to stab me so the two of you can elope?"

"Funny. She left a few minutes ago," Rocco said.

Right about this time, the doorman buzzed announcing my mom's arrival.

"Here we go," I said, and exhaled.

Rocco stared at me and smiled. "It's going to be fine. She's your mom. She's awesome."

My mom arrived and after giving her a tour of my and Rocco's home, we opened a bottle of wine and played cards for a few hours. After she beat Rocco and me out of about twenty bucks, she put the cards back in the box and said, "I'm so exhausted. I barely slept last night. For some reason, I was so nervous about coming this time."

"Huh. That's weird. I wonder why," I said and shrugged my shoulders. Of course, the mature thing to do would have been to tell her that I was a mess mere seconds before she knocked on my door. But what can I say? I had the maturity of a fourteen-year-old.

"I think I'm going to go take a shower and just unwind. Would you mind if we stayed in tonight?"

"Not at all," I said, relieved. "There are towels in the linen closet."

My mom grabbed a towel out of the closet and went to her bedroom. Rocco stood in the kitchen and sipped on my vodka soda. I went over and hugged him. I figured it was the least that I could do.

"Thanks for today," I said.

"You're welcome. You sure are a whole bag of crazy, you know that, right?" Rocco said as he squeezed me.

"Yeah, I know," I said as I relaxed into his hug.

"No, seriously. You're crazy. You need to start taking some kind of pills or something for that," he said and then laughed.

"Come on, let's go sit. I've been working all day," I said in my usual sarcastic way. Thankfully, he actually liked my sarcasm. I grabbed Rocco by the hand and we plopped down on our couch. *Finally, a moment to relax.* The house didn't look like we were hoarders. No drag queens or go-go dancers popped by to say hi. Everything was as it should be.

That is, until my mom walked out of the bathroom. She stood in the hallway of the condo wearing a bathrobe with a towel draped over her shoulder—a towel that had "cum towel" written in bold lettering on it.

"Robert, do you have that hair dryer that I left at your old apartment? I didn't bring one," she said. Rocco and I stared at my mom with our mouths wide open.

"What?" my mom asked. "Oh come on, my hair doesn't look that scary, guys!" she joked.

"Um, let me get you the hair dryer and a new towel," I said.

"Oh, this towel is fine. You know me, I don't want you to have to do more laundry after I leave. I'll use this one," she said.

Rocco downed my vodka soda like he was a diabetic that was in desperate need of his juice.

"Where did you get that one? It looks like one of Rocco's gym towels?" I said, not completely sure if I was making a statement or asking a question.

"It was in your linen closet," my mom explained.

"Oh, it was, was it?" I said and turned to look at Rocco, who shot up and went to the kitchen.

"Let me get you a new one. You don't want to use his gym towel. That's gross," I said. I heard the ice cubes hitting Rocco's glass as I walked into the hallway to grab my mom a fresh towel. I opened the linen closet and the first towel I saw was the smaller towel that Ms. X sent to us. I grabbed it and threw it to the back of the closet. Nestled snugly between two stacks of towels was the *Gidget the Midget* porn that Ms. X sent to us. My mom had to have seen it. *Oh my God.* I almost passed out in the hallway. I hid my face behind the cabinet door, handed my mother a fresh towel, and snatched the crass one off of her shoulder. It still makes me queasy to this day knowing my mother was walking around with a "cum towel" draped across her shoulder as if it were fine Egyptian cotton. "Did you find the hair dryer?" my mom asked.

"It may be in the other bathroom. I'll bring it in to you," I said with my hand on the hair dryer. The truth was that I needed a moment to collect myself. I grabbed the hair dryer and put it on her bed while she was in the bathroom washing her face. I darted to the kitchen, where by this point Rocco was drinking just straight vodka. I grabbed it out of his hand.

"What do you think you're doing?" I said angrily.

"I'm sorry, I panicked," he said.

"No, you're drinking all of my vodka. Get your own drink. This is mine," I said nervously. "The 'cum rag' was sitting right out in the open for my mother to see."

"The hallway light wasn't on. She probably didn't even notice. Come on, there's no way she could have. What person in their right mind would grab a towel that said 'cum towel' on it and walk around her son's apartment with it on her shoulder?" Rocco said, trying to calm me down. Then he paused and said, "How could she not see that?"

"I don't know, Rocco," I said through clenched teeth. "What I do know is that the *Gidget the Midget* porno was also in plain view. Who could miss that? For God's sake, it reads 'They're short, they're sweet, and they're horny!' right on the package," I said and downed a giant gulp of vodka. "She had to have seen that! You couldn't miss it. It's almost as if it was intentionally put there for someone to find." I tilted my head and looked at him.

"Don't start. No way would she have done that," Rocco said.

"Oh, Eva would absolutely do that. She's going down the next time she comes in."

"That's it. I'm going to bed," Rocco said. Whenever Rocco didn't feel like dealing with something, he went to bed, assuming that everything would be clearer in the morning. This was the one time that I wanted to go with him, but couldn't.

"But wait!" I said in a very loud whisper.

"Nope, I've had enough of your insanity for one day. I'm going to bed. You figure it out," he said and then kissed my forehead. "Good night."

So I thought I'd do what I do best in awkward situations. Nothing. I grabbed my drink and sat down on one end of the large sectional couch. My mom sat on the other end and sipped her glass of wine while she paged through an old *People* magazine.

"I should do this more often," she said.

"Mom, you already do come to New York pretty often," I said and laughed.

"No, have a glass of wine every now and then at home. I don't know why I don't."

"You totally should. Senior-citizen alcoholism is very trendy," I said.

"And apparently so are smart-ass kids," she said and then laughed.

The truth was that I was actually the one who was slightly buzzed. To distract from this, I turned on the television.

"What do you want to watch?" I asked.

"It doesn't matter to me. I'm probably going to go to bed soon," she said.

It was just like I was sitting on the couch back in my parents' house. It felt as normal as it should. Whether it was the giant cup of vodka and soda or simply my mom's presence, I was relaxed and I finally realized that all of this stress was for naught. What did I think would happen? After all we'd gone through together. I was an idiot and thankfully she never discovered any of Ms. X's gifts. I stared blankly at the TV and continued to flip channels until I landed on a show I didn't recognize but my mom did.

"Wait, stay on this one. Oh my God, I haven't seen this in years. I didn't even know that they played reruns of this old show anymore," she said and suddenly perked up.

I studied the TV, trying to figure out what we were watching. I thought I had a pretty good database of television shows stored in my brain.

"I have no idea what it is," I said.

"That's Sally Field. Don't you recognize her? She's *Gidget*," my mom said.

I had a flash of the little person version of Gidget and my panic momentarily returned. Then, I looked back at Sally Field on the beach and realized the Gidget I envisioned was leagues away from the person my mom was thinking about. I relaxed back into the couch.

My mom continued, "I used to love her when I was a kid. I wanted to be her," she said and smiled.

"You did, Mom?"

"I did." She paused and without missing a beat, my mother said, "The Sally Field *Gidget,* not the one you have in your closet."

Mama Says

As a teen of the late sixties, I loved watching the *Gidget* movies and the short-lived television show. Like the show's title character, I was also a "little girl with BIG ideas" and would tell anyone that would listen.

Gidget and I had a lot in common, especially our fiery personality. As my mom and dad frequently told people, I always had to have the last word. They weren't entirely wrong. Whenever I was told to do something, I always asked "Why?" This likely drove my parents absolutely nuts. Perhaps, just maybe, this is where Robert gets his stubbornness. Gidget and I also shared the same spirit for adventure and passion to do anything that boys liked to do. While the other girls my age learned how to sew or put on makeup, I mowed the yard, pulled weeds, waterskied, and swam. I think that's why I took to the character of Gidget as much as I did.

Gidget never liked to be told that something was for boys only and neither did I. So when I was told that I couldn't apply for a lifeguard position at the local swimming hole because I was a girl I did what I always did, I asked why. The people at the parks and recreation office wouldn't give me a straight answer and eventually the park manager tried to tell me that they weren't hiring, even though I knew through my friends that they were. I wasn't about to take no for an answer.

I begged the manager to give me a chance, but he ignored my pleading. Instead, I showed up every day and swam alongside the boys. He still didn't budge. He also conveniently forgot that I took lifesaving lessons for four years in a row and that I passed all the required tests the very first time around. It still didn't matter to him, but he also didn't know my conviction. I was never one to be told no. I continued to go every day to spite him and to prove myself. I taught swimming lessons to kids and even some parents until finally he agreed to let me try out for the position. Gidget and I were soul sisters.

The day of my tryout, I blew away the boys in all areas of the agility and lifesaving tests. There was no denying that I was the most qualified person for the job and the manager had no choice but to let me lifeguard that summer. I was the only girl who even thought of applying for the job. My parents couldn't believe it. They knew I was tenacious, but this was beyond their expectations. When I would later retell this story to friends and family, they'd often use words like "revolutionary" or "feminist." I was a young girl from a very small town and didn't realize that an entire woman's movement was happening throughout the rest of the country. I just knew what was fair and what wasn't and that principle has guided me through much of my life today.

As crazy as it sounds, I often dreamed of living in a big city like Paris when I grew up, like Gidget did. In some ways, she was my alter-ego, someone that I could live vicariously through. Yet Paris wasn't in the cards for me and, after my pregnancy, my life plan changed as life plans often do. However, I remember as I let go of one dream, another dream of a family was beginning. I vowed to myself that I would enjoy my life to the fullest in every way possible . . . just like my Gidget.

Decades later, as Robert was about to graduate from college he announced that he was moving to New York. I immediately recognized that same "Gidget-esque" sparkle in his eye. It's the same one that I had. He was bound and determined to be where he felt he belonged, much like I was certain that I was meant to sit in that lifeguard chair. It wouldn't have mattered if we tried to convince him otherwise, this kid was going with or without our blessing.

I was secretly jealous yet so proud of him for having the guts to do something out of his comfort zone. He always wanted to go to a big city and he proved that he could do it. However, I knew that Robert wouldn't be the only member of the family to enjoy the excitement of big city life. I would also experience the thrill of walking the streets of Manhattan. I relished when other tourists would stop and ask *me* for directions or when we went to restaurants and they remembered us. In some ways, I had the New York City adventure without actually having to live there.

He's shared a lot of his life and stories with me and I am incredibly happy for him and feel blessed that he's made me a part of it. I still love it when I visit NYC because I never know what I am going to discover about myself. Who knew that after so many years I'd still feel that special connection to Gidget? So maybe I was living the Gidget dream after all . . . just not the "other" Gidget that I found that night in Robert's linen closet.

CHAPTER TWENTY

No-Pudge Brownies

Delicious brownies that are only two points on the Weight Watchers system; or, what I was making when my mother dropped a bombshell

One of the many things that my mother and I have in common is our love of chocolate. It doesn't matter if it's in cakes, cookies, coffee, or brownies. If it has that thick, chewy, chocolaty taste, we will attack it. Sadly, we both had a huge problem on our hands. Weight Watchers didn't allow for our chocolate binges. My mother was determined to find a remedy to this dilemma.

I'd become a CNN junkie and was staring mindlessly at the TV when she called to tell me about her newest discovery, a fat-free brownie that actually tasted like real chocolate, as opposed to the typical cardboard-flavored treats I'd grown accustomed to in the last few months.

"No-Pudge" brownies sounded like the answer to my prayers. I quickly hung up and ran to the store to buy my box of chocolate bliss. That's the beauty of living in New York. You can get anything you want, 24/7. I found the No-Pudge mix nestled in between my former lovers, Nestle and Pillsbury. The pig on the front of the box gave me serious pause. I already felt like a fatty standing at the checkout line with three boxes of ice cream sandwiches and Diet Coke. Now this? The cashier was judging me; I could feel it.

I made it back just in time for Larry King.

Pat, an evangelical minister, was denouncing the "homosexual agenda" in America to Larry. Pat was grim-looking, with a forehead full of wrinkles from a lifetime of frowning at the big agenda the gays were planning. His white shirt that was buttoned to the top unfortunately didn't cut off enough oxygen to render him unconscious.

"These gays are smart today, and they use a tactic known as 'conversion' to win support," he declared in a thick Southern drawl. He was the kind of guy who said swimming "peeyule" instead of pool. Normally I found it strangely attractive, but in Pat's case I was getting more of a *Deliverance* vibe. Apparently part of the gay "conversion" was an organized effort that involved a psychological attack spread through the media in shows like *Oprah* and, at that time, the *Ellen DeGeneres Show*—the sitcom, not the talk show. (If he only knew that the only thing most gay men can organize is a party, he'd save a lot of money on anti-wrinkle cream.)

He was too ridiculous, and I was just about to shut him off when Pat started a brand-new assault, one so scary to me that I put the "No-Pudge" box down immediately and stood motionless in front of the television.

For years now, Disney was a name associated with apple pie, baseball, and the American way. But folks, wake up! The world is going to hell in a handbasket thanks to Walt Disney. They have launched an attack on American families everywhere by folding to the gay agenda, Pat shouted. Even Larry wasn't sure what to make of his tirade.

It was one thing to say gay people are going to hell or eternal damnation or some other place that a gay bar would quickly snatch up the name to, but to insult my Disney was blasphemous. From ages seven to thirteen, my mother hauled us to Walt Disney World in the blistering Florida sun during one of the hottest months of the year so her kids could invade the Magic Kingdom like every other kid.

When I was eight, we'd spent two blistering days without meeting a single happy Disney character. Sure, the rides were okay, but we had gone there to meet Mickey and the crew. My mother began to feel dissension in the ranks. It wasn't obvious, but she could tell.

When she would ask one of us what we thought of the theme park, a resounding "fine" was heard from my brother, sister, and me. "Fine" is the last word that should ever leave a person's lips at Disney World. Later, while coming down from an Icee high, my mom came into the hotel room with a glaze over her eyes holding five tickets in her hands. Her hair was wild, as were her eyes. I quickly inched toward the window, in case I needed to escape should she open fire.

"You want to see some characters?" she said, her voice shaking. (My mother never could yell; her voice always cracked, making her sound like a frog in heat.) "I'll show you some characters!" She then threw the tickets on the bed. The tickets, we later learned, were to the Disney Character Breakfast, where, for two months of mortgage payments, a family was allowed to eat a poorly catered breakfast of runny eggs and grits with Disney characters parading around. It was genius!

Dressed in sky-blue shorts, a Goofy T-shirt, gym socks pulled to just below my knees, and the appropriate sun visor, I was a fashion disaster at eight years old. Yet I prepared myself to meet Disney royalty. My sister and brother ditched me for the very un-Disneyesque tradition of trying to buy beer as a pre-teenager in the convenience store parking lot across the street, while I was left in the care of my mother and grandmother.

I stared at the toast on my plate while Tigger from *Winnie the Pooh* was jumping around the room, table to table. My grandmother began singing along to "It's a Small World," which played quietly over the restaurant's stereo system. I sank deeper into my seat as Tigger danced his striped ass off for the other tables, but never once did he come to ours. As he began to walk out of the room, I heard my mother shout, "What about our table?" The feline turned and shrugged before he left. I would have been happy just to skip the meal and go bust my brother and sister trying to buy beer. That would have been entertainment! My mother glanced at me and saw me smiling through my disappointment.

"I'll be back in a minute," she said, excusing herself from the table. My grandmother was now on to singing the theme from *The Mickey Mouse Club*. Within a few minutes, my mother returned to our table followed by true Disney royalty: Mickey, Minnie, and Donald. To this day, I still don't know what she did to get them, but that was my mother. She wanted to make sure that I got the same experience as every other kid.

From then on, Disney World was a sacred institution to me, and as I sat on my sofa, some guy from the Concerned Christian Family Research Council for America, or something like that, was blasting the new gay agenda at Disney. "Disney is one of the leading promoters of the homosexual lifestyle, as well as the homo political and social agenda that is spreading quicker than AIDS in a bathhouse," he argued. "Disney's gay agenda must be stopped, and I call on a nationwide boycott of the company," he added. I wasn't sure what bothered me more, the horrible stack of lies this fundamentalist was spewing or the fact that I didn't know that I had been invited to be a part of a new gay Disney agenda, as I'd been such a loyal supporter for so long.

This was the one time I was happy for a commercial break. I got up and went back to making my brownies. I felt pathetic. Not only did I feel like this guy had robbed me of a good night watching Larry King and enjoying some chocolate; he scared the shit out of me when I realized he was not alone in his beliefs. He told Larry he had almost two and a half million supporters. That was enough hate to silence ten times that number of gays and lesbians, I thought. I had just grabbed the box of "No-Pudge" when my phone rang.

Lightly spray an 8×8-inch pan with cooking spray.

"Aren't they delicious?" my mother asked.

"Just started," I said.

"Are you at least mixing yet?" she asked.

"No, I'm almost there. By the way, did you see Larry King tonight?" I asked bitterly.

"Now what?"

"Just some idiot," I said. "Gay people get the short end of the stick on everything." I didn't really mean to be so extreme, but I somehow felt like one of those rainbow flag, pink triangle–carrying guys I cringed at growing up when watching the nightly news. They made me uneasy when dealing with my own reality. As much as I abhorred them, I loved them for speaking out, because I knew I was too scared to do so. The truth was, my life had been pretty amazing up until now, thanks to my wonderful family, and no American Family Research organization was going to tell me otherwise, let alone tell me I had a "depraved mind."

Add ⅔ cup nonfat vanilla or French vanilla yogurt and mix to blend. The batter will be very thick.

"That's as ridiculous as the minister you're talking about. I got news for you—being judged or discriminated against comes in all forms and is not exclusive to being gay," she argued. I could hear the anger growing in her voice, but for some reason I continued to push, because I knew that, unlike at Disney World, this was one case where she couldn't make sure that her kid got the same treatment as everyone else.

"I know, but come on. Can you honestly name a time that as a heterosexual you've ever been discriminated against because of your sexuality?" I asked.

Once the dry mix is incorporated, stir well for about a minute until the batter is smooth and shiny.

"Actually, I can. When I was pregnant with your brother, I was judged and discriminated against."

"Because you had him at a young age. But besides idle gossip, nothing major happened to you. Big deal! I had to hide who I was for twenty-one years and face teasing and torment my whole life." Somehow my anger toward the moron on CNN had taken a wrong turn.

Pour into the prepared pan and bake for 32–34 minutes.

There was a long pause. I knew I'd crossed the line. Had I been home, I'd have felt a quick smack across my mouth, as was customary whenever I tested the waters. Finally, she said quietly, "I wasn't allowed to attend my senior year of high school because I was pregnant."

Much like my brownies in the oven, my perception of my mother and her "easy" life had just been burned.

Mama Says

One thing I've learned about life is that at one time or another, everyone thinks they're the only human being on the planet who has been wronged by somebody else. The truth is that it happens to us all: gay or straight. Unfortunately, it's usually the same type of person who does the judging.

Getting pregnant at seventeen in 1967 in a small Midwestern town was all you would ever imagine it to be. I don't have to set the stage and explain just how nasty people can be, because Lifetime Television has covered enough of those situations, but let's just say that it was all that and then some. I was the last person people thought would get pregnant in high school. I had big plans—go to college, have a career, *then* get married and start a family, in that order. But life doesn't always work out the way you planned, as so many of us learn.

At the time, I was feeling so many different emotions, especially embarrassment and fear. (I hated to babysit as a kid, and now here I was about to have one of my own.) My biggest obstacle, or so I thought, was telling my parents. In a small community, it's hard to keep a secret. I tried at first but then realized it was useless, as a big belly would be headed my way within a matter of months. Much like Robert, I worried that I'd bring shame to my family because of something that was a part of me. My father was an important businessman in town. How was it going to look when his youngest daughter was unmarried and pregnant? I had to "come out" to my parents, so to speak, because the clock was ticking.

Before I could sit my parents down and tell them the news, my mother came to me and told me she knew I was pregnant. It was one of those things that mothers just "know," even though I hadn't started to show. My mother made it clear to me that I didn't have to get married, but I did because even as scared as I was, I loved Ron. My father was beyond disappointed in me and the situation. He even told me he didn't think the marriage would last. Thirty-seven years later we're still together, but my parents divorced after twenty-three years of marriage. My dad later remarried and stayed with his new wife for thirty-three years, until he recently passed away. So here I was, the girl who everyone thought would be divorced within a few years, and I've outlasted them all.

However, I quickly learned that telling my parents wouldn't be my only obstacle. Gossip quickly spread throughout town and my life suddenly became very hard. My parents bore the brunt of the gossip, much as Ron and I did about Robert. It's never easy to hear people talk about your children; it's like the feeling you get when you walk into a room and suddenly everyone stops talking, except it's continuous. My parents stood behind me, but inside it was tearing all of us apart.

They called me into our living room and told me they needed to talk to me. I could see the hurt in my mother's eyes. The school had notified them that I wouldn't be allowed to return to school. I would have to complete my last year of high school at home. I was devastated. I had gone from being one of the more popular girls to the town pariah. I had a lot of tears at home, but I'd never show it in public. I always maintained my dignity. Even at seventeen, I told myself that each person has his or her own path in life. If the high school administration's journey included ignorance and prejudice toward me, that was their issue. Trying to change their opinion or make them understand wasn't my job. My life was my job.

I continued to make my life my job by doing the same amount of schoolwork as everybody else. My guidance counselor sent my work home each week. I had double the work as both teacher and student, but surprisingly I received some of the highest marks I'd ever had.

My classmates voted me homecoming queen that year, which for most young women would be the highlight of their high school experience, but for me it was painfully ironic. I wasn't allowed to either attend the ceremonies or accept the crown, by order of the school administrators. These complete strangers judged me without having one conversation with me. I had feelings, hopes, dreams just like every other person, but it didn't matter, because I was different and they didn't want to send the "wrong message" to the rest of the students (as if they were going to get pregnant by looking at me). Instead, they crowned my best friend, Linda, the same night as my wedding rehearsal dinner. Now that was tough.

At the end of the year, when our yearbooks arrived, I couldn't wait to have all my friends sign mine before they went off to college. My guidance counselor had sent mine along with my schoolwork, and just as I was about to leave to have it signed, I flipped through the pages to make sure my picture didn't look too silly. I was never one to take a good school picture, so I wanted to be sure I didn't look like a complete dork. I flipped through my class and I couldn't find my picture anywhere. At first, I thought I'd skimmed by too quickly and overlooked it. Then I looked through the rest of the yearbook and noticed that several of my pictures had been removed. It was as if I hadn't existed. I'd been erased just as easy as that. It frightens me even to this day how easily people in positions of power can corrupt and destroy so much in the blink of an eye. I cried for weeks until my tears turned into anger. I eventually got my guidance counselor on the phone and told him that if he wanted a war, the school would get one, because I was not about to be treated like a second-class citizen any longer. He took me seriously enough to include my photo in the yearbook the following year, which is why I've encouraged all my kids never to let anyone rob them of their life experiences or their joy. Sometimes, you just have to stand up and fight, even when you feel as though you just can't win.

High school ended and a few of my friends tried to stay in touch, but only for a while, and they soon faded. After I finished high school, I moved to Bloomington, where Ron was going to college. I took several college courses, but with a family, I knew college would have to wait, and unfortunately it's still waiting.

Robert is a lot like me. We both had something to tell and we both survived. Only I think I got off a little easier than him. The crimes and hate against gay people are terrifying. It's gotten better, but it exists, which is so wrong. So many fundamentalist groups that disguise themselves as "family" groups incite hate toward others. They weren't organized when I was a teenager, yet I still felt their hate for not being a part of their moral code.

Over the years, I have come to believe that my purpose in life is to raise a good family, be a good mother and grandmother, and, most of all, be a good wife. I feel I've done that. When I accepted that I wasn't going to go to college and have a career, life became easier; the pressure was off. Robert often points out to me when I'm feeling down, "Mom, you are a fantastic person. You don't need college to say who you are. Your actions speak volumes." I've had a great life. All the kids went to college, graduated with honors, and have good jobs. What more could I ask for?

For some, their purpose in life is to be good at what they have in front of them. My family is my life, and being a constant in their lives is my purpose. I am extremely proud of my family, and thanks to them, I'm pretty damn proud of myself, too.

CHAPTER TWENTY-ONE
M'Lynn Moment

Based on the Sally Field character in *Steel Magnolias* and her fit of despair and depression at her daughter Shelby's funeral

As clichéd as it sounds, it's true what people say: Your life flashes before you in the blink of an eye when you're near death. I never really understood how that could be possible, because up until now I had such a full life, plus I blink really fast.

I lay in the emergency room at St. Luke's Roosevelt and thought I was going to die. My lung had collapsed—spontaneously, according to my doctor. Apparently, my left lung had gotten bored of the monotony of breathing in and out and said, "To hell with it. I'm going on strike."

I watched as doctors shoved an oxygen tube up my nose, hooked a heart monitor to my chest, and continually checked my vitals. I waited for the movie of my life to begin playing in my head, like I'd heard about on so many daytime talk shows. I contemplated writing a letter to psychic Sylvia Browne to complain. The beeping noise on my heart monitor got quicker with each minute that passed. The nurse rushed over to my bed and stood over me checking me once again. I tried to tell her that the reason my heart was beating so fast was that the noise from the heart monitor was scaring the hell out of me. But I was too weak to talk. Instead, I closed my eyes in silent protest.

Within minutes, a doctor came to my bedside, grabbed my hand, and asked me to squeeze. I looked at him and had a vision of him and me finishing our dinner at Moomba together. Even on death's door, I was trying to score a date. He then asked me a series of questions. I thought it was because he was interested, but my mother later explained that he was trying to see if I was coherent.

As he began talking, I drifted off into another daydream. Yet instead of my *own* life, for some reason my thoughts went immediately to the movie *Steel Magnolias*. (As a gay man, it's on your list of required viewing.) My mind skipped through all the useless back story and straight to the pivotal scene in the film where Truvy, Ouiser, Annelle, and Clairee try to comfort M'Lynn after her daughter Shelby has died. At first she's strong, but as she walks back to her car, she loses it. I heard the heart monitor going sporadic just as M'Lynn was in a full-on wail. The nurses rushed around me while I kept replaying that scene, wondering if someone had loved me that deeply. Of course, I knew my parents loved me, but was it the kind of love that inspired a M'Lynn moment?

The heart monitor shot up even faster, and my thoughts finally left Sally Field and Shirley MacLaine and went to my parents. My own life finally began to play in my head. *This must be it for me*, I thought. I was going to have to send Sylvia Browne an apology from the other side. The hospital room disappeared before me, and all I saw were memories and flashes of my family. It was like watching a movie in fast forward.

Random memories started filling my head. I remembered my father begrudgingly waiting for what seemed like hours at McDonald's for my special plain cheeseburgers. I remembered my mom taking me to see Michael Jackson in concert. I remembered my parents packing me up for my move to New York. Flashes of life and the people that filled it continued to swirl in my head. I thought about my mother and our daily Weight Watchers phone calls. I thought about Diane, the crazy group leader, telling me I was still a lil' chubby. I thought about singing karaoke with my nieces and nephews over the holidays.

I remember saying out loud, "Oh, my God. I get this now. This is what this is like." Whether it was truly my life flashing before my eyes or just the IV kicking in, I'll never know. One thing was for sure—I was freaking the nurses out.

With tubes coming out my nose, wires covering my chest, and an IV hooked up to my arm, I couldn't escape the thought that this would be the last image my parents saw of their son. I thought I was going to die, and what's worse, it was just as my mother had feared, alone. Tears began to burn the side of my face as I lay quietly in the chaos around me.

After they stuck a tube in the side of my chest to pump my lung back up, I was hauled off to intensive care, where I stayed for three days. Not surprisingly, my mother was at my side the following day. For the next seven days, she was at the hospital the very second visiting hours began and had to be practically carried out each night by the nurses.

With a stubborn lung that wouldn't pump back up, I was utterly depressed. This was the kind of scenario in which I always imagined a boyfriend holding a vigil next to my hospital bed. Since Rocco and I had called it quits a few months earlier, I had plenty of time to deal with my own issues of solophobia.

Knowing me as only a mother could, she stopped at the deli every morning and brought me a sugar cookie the size of my hand in lieu of hospital food. It was exactly the medicine I needed. Weight Watchers went out the window, and we laughed as we tallied the amount of points for each cookie. I slowly began to recover, and to this day, I truly believe that if she hadn't been there, it would have taken a great deal longer.

As I grew stronger physically, emotionally I reached a new resolve. I finally realized that I might never find a boyfriend, let alone a life partner, and that was okay. Nobody said it better than Carrie Bradshaw in her last lines in *Sex and the City*: "The most exciting, challenging, and significant relationship of all is the one you have with yourself. And if you find someone who loves the you you love, that's just fabulous."

The night before I was scheduled to be released, *Steel Magnolias* was on TV. I lay in the hospital bed and looked at my mother, who was falling asleep in her chair. I realized how much this woman had done for me. She loved me unconditionally, whether gay or straight. Above all else she was a mother, and I was her son—the rest were just details. She began to snore as my eyes welled up with tears. I reached for the remote and turned the movie off. I was having my own version of a M'Lynn moment.

Mama Says

While I was on the first plane out of town to get to Robert's bed-side, I had plenty of time to think about how much he meant to me and our family. He always has a smile on his face, always happy and always trying to make everyone around him feel comfortable. He has a zest for life like no one I have ever seen. Knowing that he was lying in a hospital all alone, it broke me up. My flight couldn't land fast enough. His dad wanted to be there, but he was working and we weren't sure of the severity of the situation or how long I needed to be there.

During the flight, I thought about him always telling me that I needed to be more independent and be able to navigate New York by myself. I love flying and traveling, but big cities can scare me sometimes. I repeatedly told him that I would always be either with him or his dad when I was in Manhattan, so why bother? I laughed to myself while I sat in my seat. That little shit. I was going to have to get into his apartment and over to the hospital all by myself. On my last trip to visit I finally was used to getting a cab alone. I had a feeling that there was a part of him that was secretly enjoying the fact that I had to stare down some of my biggest fears. I'm not sure why I was worried, I raised three kids and made it through. I can sure as hell get around without Robert's help, I thought.

When I arrived at the hospital, he was sound asleep with a heart monitor on, an IV, and a tube coming from between his ribs. I was relieved to see him resting because when he woke up he would see his mother there waiting to see what the hell had happened to him.

Both the nurse and doctor filled me in on what was going on and told me that things could have been much worse if the door-man at his apartment building hadn't seen him collapse and called 911. I felt a sinking feeling in my stomach. I hadn't realized just how severe things were. Finally, after going through all the details, I received the news he was going to be okay. I let out a big sigh of relief and I was ready to take care of my youngest child again. Robert woke up and had a big smile on his face. With the kind of sheep-ish smile that only Robert can give, he looked at me and asked how I did getting around New York. I told him that I did just fine with-out him. I wasn't about to admit that I went to the wrong hospital at first.

Within a day or so, Robert was starting to feel much better. I knew this only because he asked me if I wouldn't mind getting him some cookies from the bakery across the street from the hospital. He is a lot like me in that way: Give us something sweet and we will feel better soon no matter what the situation. Over the next several days, I got to know the people at the bakery and they usu-ally had his cookie waiting for me when I walked in. As I waited in line to pay, I looked around at so many of the different faces in the bakery. Most were familiar faces that I had seen walking in the lobby of the hospital. I assumed that many were family members or friends visiting loved ones. It got me thinking about the frailty and complexity of life.

When we get down to the nitty-gritty things in our life, we all have had to deal with some tough situations. Your problems may not be as bad as the next guy, but it doesn't mean they don't exist. And when you think nobody in the world could possibly have it worse off than you at that very moment and you're going through pain that seems unimaginable, open your mouth and talk to someone else because chances are, they've gone through worse. You're not the first to have pain, and you won't be the last.

It's amazing how we can torture ourselves into believing that our problems are insurmountable. Robert realized when his lung collapsed and he spent a week in the hospital that his family was with him every step of the way. For me, his being gay is the last thing that entered my mind; I simply didn't want to lose my son. Since Robert has come out I have been much more vocal on gay rights. Robert tries to explain a lot of the rights to me and what should be happening with the government concerning gay rights. I understand some of it, but I compare it to when Robert played tennis in high school: I didn't understand it fully but I kept at it and continued to support him through every last match.

Bottom line: We all need to pull it together and get along—life is way too short.

CHAPTER TWENTY-TWO

Mother's Gay

Nobody knows of the work it makes
to keep the home together. Nobody knows of the steps it takes
nobody knows but mother.
—Anonymous

Nobody knows the messes I make but my mother.
—Robert Rave

From: Robert Rave
Sent: May 6 11:21:23
Subject: HAPPY MOTHER'S GAY

Sorry, I can't make it home this weekend for Mother's Day.
Trying to get everything organized for my move to LA has
been more of a nightmare than I originally imagined. I would
have invited you here for Mother's Day, but who am I
kidding? I would have put you to work organizing everything and you would have demanded that I take you for
cosmopolitans—every night.

I can't believe that it was ten years ago that I came out
to you. Actually, I can't believe that I'm thirty-one. You
realize I'm virtually irrelevant in the gay community at this
age, don't you? I kid, I kid. But seriously, I am currently
looking for a good Botox guy. Maybe you can go too when
you come for your next visit.

Anyway, back to Mother's Day or in this case Mother's
Gay—since you are, in fact, the most kick-ass mother of a
gay. I have to say that you handled my coming out with

such utter grace and love. You didn't waver in your support of me and that has helped make me the man I am today. It also saved me a fortune on therapy, so for that alone I thank you.

In some ways, I feel like I came out to you last week. I can still remember when you playfully scolded me for not telling you sooner and then for making the genius move of mailing you and Dad a letter instead of calling. I never claimed to be your smartest child.

We both felt the pressures of staying fit and looking good even when we wanted to reach for a giant piece of chocolate cake. Don't get me started on those damn points. For years, I couldn't go anywhere without calculating everything in my head. I was some kind of point "Rain Man." It wasn't pretty.

I realized that not only did I come out to you, I took you *out*—on the town. I'm proud to say that you had your first cosmopolitan with me. And your second, your third, and then fourth, in the same night I might add. However, I was so delighted to see a group of my New York City friends as well as total strangers be able to experience how exactly amazing my small-town, Midwestern mother was.

You listened to me complain about the men I dated, something I never in my wildest dreams as a closeted young boy would have imagined talking to my mother about. You tried pointing out guys to me that you thought would make a good match for me—even though some looked like serial killers. You even threatened to have "a talk" with a jerk that broke my heart. You came to visit my boyfriend and me at our new home and didn't bat an eyelash.

You also weren't afraid to tell me when my neurosis was getting the best of me, which during my twenties, and sometimes even now, is a lot. You bailed me out of serious credit card debt. You debated waxing with the rest of the family as it pertained to me. You told me that you or my friends could solve the same problems that any therapist could. I'm not sure I 100 percent agree with you on that, but your advice that I simply needed to eat more I took to heart and indulged.

You reminded me that through it all, the paramount thing to remember was to stay true to myself and be an authentic person.

I always knew that you were a pretty remarkable person, but I thought that was just how most moms were. I didn't know any different. As I've gotten older, I realize that I'm so very fortunate to have a mother like you.
Happy Mother's Day, I mean, Gay!
I love you,
Robert

Mama Says

From: Jane Rave
Sent: May 6 1:34:21
Subject: Re: HAPPY MOTHER'S GAY

Hi Robert,
Thanks for the "Mother's Gay" wishes. I think?

I wanted to drop you a note and tell you how proud I am of you about being open with your life at last. You have had a weight lifted off your shoulders and I can see it in your eyes and the even bigger smile on your face. It took a lot of courage to do what you did and I am so proud of you.

You have made me stop and think about my own life and how I need to be honest with myself and about getting married so young and feeling like a failure for getting pregnant. You would think after 43 years of marriage I would let up on myself, but I am pretty darn hard on myself.

I admire you for letting go of hiding all your feelings for being gay and not being able to tell us. I thank you so much for sharing so much of your life with me and taking me all the way to NYC and loving every minute of it.

I think we both came out, so to speak. HaHa.

I think I know you pretty well and from the tone of your
e-mail I get the feeling you are setting me up for something
else, and I am not sure what it is.
You are always up to something.

Miss you.
Dad and I will call you later in the weekend.

Love,
Mom

CHAPTER TWENTY-THREE
The Beginning

A fresh start and a new idea

I was confronted with the most difficult decision every New Yorker must face. When is it time to leave? At least two or three times a year, most New Yorkers ask themselves that very question. However, with great resolve, they forge ahead and continue to have one of the greatest addresses in the world. With eternal optimism, New Yorkers hold on to the dream of one day having the life they had always imagined when they first moved into a 550-square-foot studio apartment. A dream so few actually get to experience.

Something inside told me it was the time to make my move. If I didn't do it now, I was never going to make the break and I'd be caught in a never-ending struggle. I needed to jumpstart my career and really begin my "adult life," as my thirtieth birthday was rapidly approaching. Yet I still felt as though I was breaking up with the city I had loved so much for so long.

One of my worst fears materialized in the form of a brochure from Alternative Living for the Aging, a gay retirement village. The thought of being surrounded by a group of old queens at the "home" gossiping made me nauseous. I could hear it: "Mary, you know that queen is so randy he'd hump a doorknob if they'd let him" as old Mariah Carey dance remixes played in the activities room. I had just turned thirty, and by gay standards I'd crossed the threshold of going from "that's hot" to "that's not" as the ubiquitous Paris Hilton would say. I still had nothing significant to show for all of my work, and like any gay man I compared my accomplishments to my peers. I wasn't exactly "velvet mafia" material. Yes, it was definitely time for me to make my move. At the exact moment I made up my mind, my mother called.

"What's going on in the big city?" she asked.

"You know—just channeling my inner Truman Capote."

"Haven't written a word, huh?"

"Not one."

"Do you think I look like a lesbian?" she said. She'd often begin mid-thought, as if we'd been talking for hours. I held the retirement pamphlet in my hand and stared at the mirror.

"A lesbian? Why would you say that?" I said, examining my forehead, dreading the thought of future trips for Botox. Instead, I plotted my next trip to the "age-defying" creams counter at Saks while she continued.

"The girl at the hair salon said she thought I went too short with my haircut and I looked like a lesbian."

"You say that like it's a bad thing."

Then suddenly, after months of creative drought, an idea was born thanks to my mother's short, efficient haircut. We would write a mother/son book together, a book that would show our take on the perceptions and misconceptions of what it's like to be gay and to have a gay child. We would open a dialogue for parents and children for years to come. It was completely new and original. There was only one problem: getting my mother to say yes.

My mother had always been the type of person who protects "the family." She and the city of Las Vegas shared a similar mantra: "What happens within the family *stays* in the family." Although we're an all-American Midwestern family, you'd think she was Mama Soprano. She once excommunicated a cousin of hers for telling a mutual friend that my sister had been suspended from school for getting drunk and puking on the principal's shoes. To this day, they still don't speak. And now I wanted to write a book about our family experience. I could kiss my inheritance good-bye.

A few months later, my mother and I sat in a back corner of New York's Pastis. I immediately ordered her a coffee to make sure she had enough caffeine running through her veins in the event that the shock of my news caused her heart to stop suddenly.

I sat and watched her sip her coffee and take in the bright New York morning. Of course, *she* was in a state of bliss, drinking her coffee and waiting for her French toast. *French toast?* I thought. How could she have an appetite while my stomach churned in agony? I thought mothers were supposed to sense when their children were in crisis.

As I was about to blurt out my plan, a group of well-preened thirty-something gay men sat down at the table next to us, each one sexier and more muscular than the next. They were gay gold, and I most certainly was not. My self-esteem plummeted while my mother remained oblivious to their existence. She was content simply sipping her drink and spending a Sunday afternoon with her son.

My desperation grew, and I knew I had to act fast. Luckily, my last job as a New York City publicist provided me with excellent training in the art of manipulation. I took my last sip of espresso and finally blurted it out. "Mom, I think we should write a book together."

She slowly eased back into her chair, looked at me, shifted again anxiously, grabbed her coffee and took a giant sip, and finally responded with a laugh, "That's funny, but you know I don't write."

"Sure you can. You're hilarious," I said shakily. I found her funny, but would other people think my POWW (Prisoner of Weight Watchers) mother was, too?

"What on earth would we write about?" she asked as the waiter poured her a fresh cup. As he began to leave, she grabbed his arm forcefully and muttered, "Leave it." The nervous waiter set the coffeepot down and slowly backed away from the table.

"Well . . ." I said as the lump in my throat grew by the second. "It would be about our experiences, how you've learned about my personal life." She wasn't getting it. "We could write about . . . you know . . . how can I say this?"

"How you're gay?" she blurted.

"Bingo."

"I-I-I just don't know, Robert," she stuttered. "It's not that I'm ashamed of who you are, but I just don't know if I could do something like that. I'm very private and this . . . well, isn't."

She needed more. I quickly fired off that the book wouldn't be about only me but about the ways in which our lives had often paralleled each other's. I couldn't look at her face, so I stared at the pattern in the tile work.

"We both faced discrimination and we both overcame it." I looked up at her face, which was now flush and wet with perspiration.

"Why would you want to tell all these people about being gay? I thought you said your sexuality was no big deal," she fired off.

"I want to because it could make a difference in the life of some kid who has to live a lie," I explained.

"But why me?" she asked.

"Because you are the voice of mothers across the country who have gay children and try to understand them. You are the quintessential *Red Mom*."

"Red what?" she asked, confused.

"You're from a red state. You have conservative 'values.' You're, as Chaka Khan would say, *every woman*." My Chaka reference was met with a confused stare. I continued, "Your voice lets parents know it's okay to laugh with their kids about their sexuality, as opposed to the typical gloom-and-doom scenario."

"So, that would make you my blue son," she quipped.

"Exactly." I grinned. She stared at me long and hard while the sweat continued to run down her face. While shifting in her seat, she became fixated on the table full of very successful, hunky men next to us. She studied everything about them: their blinding white teeth, wrinkle-free perfect skin, razor-cut hair, and finally their form-fitting clothes. She looked back at me and couldn't help but look at my baggy ripped jeans and vintage "My Mom Thinks I'm a Catch" T-shirt. However, it was in that moment my mother entered *my* reality.

It was as if an imaginary checklist of all my insecurities, hopes, and dreams—not only as her son but as a gay man—were being realized. She began to understand my neurosis about my work, the pressures to stay hot and viable after thirty, and the paralyzing fear of waking up alone every day. These were universal issues, and she finally grasped their importance and my need to share *our* story with the rest of the world, even if it was at the risk of alienating not only her but the rest of my extended family by writing such an honest book.

She took a deep breath, looked me square in the eyes, and said, "If this is what you need me to do, I will do it." She had such a Machiavellian tone that even I was a little freaked out. I wasn't exactly asking her to off my agent, but since she agreed to this so easily, I thought I might be able to get away with it. Put that on my "to do" list.

I was speechless.

"It has to be authentic—no stereotypes. We will tell *our* story, not some cliché," she said matter-of-factly. Most kids would make a scrapbook for their parents. I, on the other hand, was asking her to write a book for publication.

"Can I finish my French toast now?" she asked in a huff. I looked at the ground again. "Now what?" she said, annoyed.

"I'm leaving New York," I said quietly. Her face became flushed again.

"Why would you want to leave New York?" she asked. I remained silent. "I love it here," she quickly added. One thing most New Yorkers seem to forget is that friends and family who don't live in New York never want you to leave. They subconsciously keep you there with subtle mind traps and passive-aggressive manipulations. You are their golden ticket to the best in theater, restaurants, nightlife, and of course, the New Yorkers' summer ritual, the Hamptons. Why would they want to give that up? You are their connection to a world they only read about or see on TV. I explained that it wasn't in fact about her, and that more job opportunities would present themselves to *me*, and while she understood my need for a change, she wasn't ready to discuss two possibly life-changing decisions in one breakfast.

While she took her last sip of coffee, I caught her saying under her breath, "I don't know why you didn't write me a letter about this one. Telling me you're gay is letter worthy; moving three thousand miles away and wanting me to write a book with you apparently isn't." She shook her head and gave me a giant smile.

Two months later the writing had begun, and I received a phone call late one morning.

"I've been doing some research on the sexual practices of gays. You're not into water sports, are you?" Research? Where in the hell was she researching water sports? However, before I could get a word out of my mouth, she followed with, "Would you consider yourself a bossy bottom?"

"The only water sports I'm into, Mother, involve a pair of skis, but thank you for the concern. How's the writing coming along?"

"Good. I have a few suggestions," she said with a hint of an ego.

"Wait a second. Do I seem like a bossy bottom to you?" I asked.

"The book?" she said, clearly not wanting to know my preferences in sexual positions.

"Give it to me," I said as I began to pace around my pint-sized apartment.

"I think we should cover your regular waxing visits."

"You wanna talk about my waxing? Are you insane?" I said, horrified. "Mom, I was thinking more along the lines of what it's like to be gay, told from a mother-and-son perspective."

"Been there, read that. You want people to buy this or not?" she shot back. "We have to cover everything, 'manscaping' and all." I was sickened that my mother had uttered the phrase "manscaping." "I've read that most men who wax usually do it to please their partner. Are you waxing for you or for someone else?"

Oh, God. What had I done? Within a matter of a few months, my mother had become a cross between the next Betty DeGeneres and "sex grandma" Sue Johanson.

What had started out as a way of getting another creative project off the ground quickly turned into a labor of love. As I wrote, I realized that even if the book never saw the light of day, at least I got to know my mother in an entirely new way, not only as a mother, but as a human being.

Fittingly, she phoned me as I was on my way to the airport to start my new life in Los Angeles.

"It never fails. She did it again," she said, irritated.

"Who did what?"

"The receptionist from the salon," she continued. "She told me I looked like a lesbian again."

"Mom, what did you say?" I asked.

"I said thank you," she said proudly.

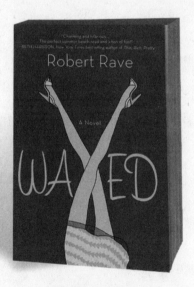